I0616350

For Sunny

Remember always caring, trying to keep me safe.
Remember always sharing, though questioning time and
place.
Remember always talking, no subject kept from view.
Remember the advice you gave, from the wisdom you knew.
At times your words were comfort — at times, a shove.
You kept me close, wrapped in tough love.
When I lacked in motion, you urged me to begin.
Eternally grateful, I've learned to earn the right to win.
When I was lonely, you held my heart and my hand.
When I said, "I can't," you said, "Char, yes you can."
Now I watch over you, keeping you safe from fears.
I see you through eyes that hold back tears.
Read these words, bold and clear, here today:
I'll always love you, each and every day.
Now I am the watcher, tugging at your heart
To let you know I'm with you, Mom.
We'll never be apart.

Before We Charge Out of the Gate

This isn't a neat timeline—it's a layered, looping ride. Sunny's fingerprints are on these pages because she never really left, even after 100 years of raising hell and holding court.

You'll tumble through chapters on swimwear retail, training philosophies, client sagas, and what it actually means to live in a body that doesn't always play nice.

Sometimes we double back before we barrel forward. It's built that way on purpose—each story sharpening the next, each truth setting up the one after.

Settle in.
Let it roll.

The Best Damn Version of You

Your Worth Doesn't Need a Stamp of Approval

For anyone who's ever felt like they don't measure up, this book says: you already do.

I've built a life that doesn't follow the blueprint.
I didn't marry. Didn't have kids. Didn't chase the version of "success" most people are taught to pursue.
Instead, I chose work that mattered.
I chose people.
I chose to show up—fully, relentlessly, without applause, and without waiting for permission.

For decades, I've been a private fitness trainer—after years of owning, running, and fitting swimwear on bodies of every shape, size, and story.

No guru status.
No brand.
No ring light or highlight reel.
Just a person who's lived inside thousands of stories, setbacks, and small wins—up close and unfiltered.

I've built a career around honesty. The kind that shows up early, prepared, focused—before the world even wakes up.
The kind that meets clients in their homes at sunrise.
That walks a retail floor scanning for problems before they happen.
The kind that doesn't knock, doesn't apologize, and won't let you look away.

Most people already have what they need to live well.
It just gets buried under noise, obligation, and insecurity.

This isn't a manual.
It's not a transformation story.
It's not a tough-love handbook telling you to get your shit together.
It's not a lecture about discipline.
And it sure as hell isn't about chasing perfection.

This is a front-row seat to the mess and the magic of being human—
Of living in a body that doesn't always cooperate,
And a mind that won't shut up.

It's a collection of real moments. Some funny. Some raw.
All true.
You'll meet people who didn't think they could keep going—
and did anyway.
You'll hear things most people are too afraid to admit, even to themselves.
You might even recognize parts of yourself you've been trying to ignore.

It's not about abs.
It's about identity.
It's not about willpower.
It's about showing up.
It's not about who you're supposed to be.
It's about who you already are.

So, if you're tired—
Tired of waiting to feel "ready." Ready for what?

Tired of putting your life on hold. For whom?
Tired of waiting for the perfect moment. When exactly?
Tired of postponing what you want. And that is...?
Tired of performing, measuring, second-guessing,
explaining, apologizing. For what? And for whose approval?

Welcome.
Not a perfect version.
Just the best damn version of you—on your terms, in your
time, for your reasons.

No pressure. Just possibility.

Let's begin.

Why I Get to Tell You This

I'm not just a trainer.
I've been the one on the hospital floor at 3 a.m.
Not for someone I barely knew—
For the woman who built me, tested me, loved me,
challenged me—
And eventually needed me more than anyone else ever had.

I've managed medications.
Wrestled with insurance reps.
Fought with doctors.
Argued with hospice coordinators.
Called out entire medical teams who should've known
better.

And then—
I've shown up to work.
On time. Focused. Counting reps. Coaching form.
Because people were depending on me.
That's the part no one claps for.

I've built strength in people who had none left.
I've walked with clients through divorce, death, diagnosis,
relapse, heartbreak, rehab, recovery—you name it.
I've heard the secrets they won't even tell their spouses.

I'm not here to preach about protein intake or six-packs.
I'm here to tell the truth.

This isn't a fitness manual.
It's a memoir with one mission—make you feel it.

A field report—written after decades in the trenches with real people, real lives, real limits, and real wins.

So, when I talk about what it takes to become the best damn version of yourself—
It's not theory.
It's not marketing.
It's not aesthetic.
It's earned.
Unfiltered.
Unapologetic.
And it's yours now, too.

Author's Note: About the Name

In 2021, I changed my name.

After spending most of my professional life known as Char—a nickname short for Charlene—I chose to take my middle name, Sandy, as my first, and my mother's maiden name, Wolf, as my last.

Why the change?

The short version: I admired my maternal side, respected the strength that came through my mother's line, and never felt tied—by marriage or meaning—to keep the name I was born with. So, I made a new one. One that felt like mine.

Many of my long-term clients still call me Char. That identity still lives in this book.
But the name on the cover—Sandy Wolf—is the one I claimed for myself.

Table of Contents

PART I: ORIGINS — SPANDEX, SWIMSUITS & STARTING OUT

Where it all began: a Brooklyn-born matriarch, a "shop", a backroom fitting space, and the early glimmer of something more. These are the roots—stitched in Lycra, folded in sarcasm, and pressed into confidence.

Chapter 1: This Wasn't in the Career Brochure

From Oberlin to swimwear retail, it was an accidental, unexpected education—body image, confidence, and real talk, one ill-lit dressing room at a time.

Before I ever corrected a squat or adjusted a deadlift, I was elbow-deep in spandex—and other people's self-esteem crises. Not coaching—fitting. Swimsuits. In a backroom with fluorescent lights that bleached out confidence faster than chlorine.

My mom, Brooklyn-born and bullshit-proof, had a sixth sense for trends before they ever hit a rack. This was pre-Amazon, pre-Lululemon—hell, before spandex was even a household word.

She set up shop in the back of a running shoe store. One hundred square feet, give or take. A sewing machine. A mirror. Maybe a prayer—and a promise not to sugarcoat anything.

She didn't open that nook dreaming of yachts or early retirement. Every dollar that came in had a destination, and a big chunk of it was aimed at getting me through college. Not just the big tuition checks that made her jaw clench when she signed them, but the smaller things nobody sees—gas to get me back and forth, books that cost more than rent, a set of sheets for a dorm bed, the occasional twenty slipped into my hand before I got on the bus.

I worked, too. Lifeguarding summers. Coaching swim teams. Taking campus jobs between classes. Grabbing winter and spring break gigs. And those loans—don't even get me started. The kind that followed you around for a decade after graduation, monthly, relentless, no excuses. But we made it work. I earned my way through, with Sunny's help. Every dollar we scraped together went somewhere, and for a while, that somewhere was me.

And what kept it all moving was the hustle in that backroom—sewing, fitting, pinning, reassuring, laughing, and sometimes consoling. Women came, word spreading that Sunny could fit a swimsuit like nobody else—and somehow, make you feel good in it.

I know. Blasphemy.

She didn't stop with women. She made suits for men. Boys. Whole swim teams. They came year-round, every season—looking for performance Lycra and a fitting that didn't feel like punishment. Eventually, she upgraded: 6,500 square feet of swimwear sanctuary, designed to look like a pool. Blue carpet floors. Dressing rooms styled like cabanas. A front desk where the bell never stopped chiming. The Washington Post did a feature. She got radio time. And customers? They came from three states away.

Once, she mailed The Washington Post a men's suit with a matching Lycra swim cap. A few days later, they called her in a panic.

"We've tried this thing on every body part," the editor said. "We're stumped. What is it?"

She laughed so hard she nearly choked on her coffee. "It's a swim cap. You put it on your head."

This was back before Lycra swim caps were even a thing. She practically invented them. The rest of the world just had to catch up.

My dad, meanwhile, had a looser definition of "achievement." He didn't build businesses. He didn't build much of anything. But he did referee swim meets. And then, somehow, landed on the Olympic Committee—just in time for the 1980 boycott. That about sums it up.

While my classmates suited up for courtrooms and corporate gigs, I held a fresh liberal arts degree—and zero clue what I wanted next. I wasn't swinging sarcasm like a sword yet. That would come in time. For now, I carried something quieter: a growing straightforwardness, a wider worldview, and the slow build of a voice that would one day slice through bullshit like a blade.

What I did need, a paycheck. Sunny didn't blink.

"You're working the store with me for now," she said. "If you find a different direction later, you'll decide then."

My professional life began in the fluorescent-lit backroom of a swimwear store. The walls were lined with suits. The floor with tape measures, pins, half-unpacked boxes, and the occasional emotional landmine.

That's where I first learned how to "train" people—long before I ever climbed on board and signed up for the role of private trainer.

And my toughest case? The one who challenged me daily, demanded precision, and never held back? My mother.

I didn't realize it at the time, but working with swimsuits and managing fittings was my first education in human psychology. Insecurity doesn't whisper—it screams. And swimsuits? They're the megaphone.

We weren't just selling swimwear—we were selling courage. Confidence. Permission. Permission to show up. To step outside. To stop hiding.

And most of the people walking through our doors? They weren't channeling Baywatch. Hell, they weren't even ready to look in the mirror.

Some walked in defensive from the second they crossed the threshold. Especially in D.C.—a city where modesty is armor and vulnerability is seen as weakness. Power suits and polished silence, yes. Visible belly fat? Not so much.

We fit hundreds—probably thousands—of women, men, boys, and girls over the years. Some were athletes. Some were grandmothers. Some were just trying to get through the season—find a swimsuit that fit, get in the water, check the box for summer, and move on.

Most leaned conservative in dress—though not always. We fit competitive swim team suits, Brazilian cuts, boxer briefs, tankinis with built-in bras, ruffled skirts, maternity pieces, mastectomy suits, and the occasional client who walked in requesting "the tightest thing you've got."

They came in for all kinds of reasons:
To hide. To cover. To compress. To distract.
But also, to accentuate. To display. To feel sexy. To be admired.

We weren't working with just "older women full of insecurities." We worked with everyone—and believe me, even the most outwardly confident ones? They had their thing.

The part of their body they didn't trust. The feature they thought betrayed them.

Insecurity isn't picky. It shows up in all shapes, sizes, ages, and income brackets.

And you know what? That taught me more about the human body than any anatomy textbook ever could. How people feel about their bodies is where the real work begins. Especially if you plan to train them. Because you can't coach someone physically if they're bracing emotionally the whole time.

Fitting people in spandex is intimate. It's personal. It's raw. It's not just chest-waist-hip measurements. It's:
• "I haven't worn a swimsuit since giving birth."
• "I gained 40 pounds during my divorce."
• "I can't look at myself in the mirror."
• "I put on 15 pounds in college and can't get rid of it."

- "I've got back hair—should I wax before the beach?"
- "My wife says these trunks are too short. Are they?"
- "Do these bottoms scream 'trying too hard,' or am I good?"

Add harsh lighting and an angled mirror, and you're holding space for a full-blown identity crisis.

You learn to read more than measurements. You learn to listen. To shut up and let someone speak. To hear the words, they don't say.

And when they ask, "How does this look?"—you don't sugarcoat. You don't sell.

You offer truth—with kindness. You remind them they're allowed to take up space.

Turns out, those are the same rules that make a damn good trainer. Show up. Tell the truth. Know your stuff. Don't fake compassion—but don't fake toughness either.

You can't help a body—or a person—if you don't respect them first.

So, by the time I started training people, I already knew what I was looking at. I knew how tension sits in the shoulders. How discomfort settles in the hips. I could clock a person's relationship with their body in five seconds flat.

And I didn't dish out empty compliments to keep the peace.

What I offered was real—specific, earned, rooted in how they moved, how they stood, how they looked at themselves.

Sometimes it was about color, or cut, or fabric. But it wasn't the comment that changed things. It was the delivery—the way I spoke to them. The way I translated what I saw into something they could actually hear.

"This neckline flatters you."
"That fabric holds and compresses without distorting."
"The waist on the trunks gives you a waist."

And slowly, they weren't quite so wary. Not quite so defensive. Relaxed? Maybe not. But grounded enough to think, This wasn't as bad as I thought. Or even: Maybe I'll come back again.

That was the work. Seeing the good, naming it with precision, and never letting the hard parts get the final say.

I didn't just come into training with a degree and a certification. I came in with years of hands-on, body-aware, emotion-loaded customer service.

Training wasn't a huge leap. It was just a different kind of transformation. Less Lycra. More lunges.

But the work? Still rooted in self-worth.

There was a pattern.

A woman would walk in, maybe twenty pounds heavier than she wanted to be. Maybe sixty. Sometimes she started talking before the door had even shut behind her.

"I just need something simple," she'd say. "Solid black. Nothing fancy."

She wasn't asking for style. She was asking for safety.

The logic? Black makes me look thinner.
The hope? Maybe I won't stand out.

I'd heard it so many times, I could predict the tone. And my response never changed:

"You're stepping into a world full of color—sun, surf, laughter, bold prints. That solid black suit? It's not hiding you. It's framing you. It becomes the background people notice because it's trying so hard not to be seen."

Instead, I'd steer her toward something with light. With balance. With quiet confidence. A neckline that lifted her face. A cut that brought shape back to her silhouette. A pattern that softened what she wanted to mute—and highlighted what she'd stopped noticing.

Color wasn't about drawing attention. It was about restoring presence. It was about control.

It was a strategy to feel more like yourself—not less.

And when it worked—when her body language eased, when her voice came back with some spark—that was the moment. That flicker of self-acceptance. That shift from self-doubt to self-possibility.

It's what kept me doing the work.

That experience—those quiet transformations in a cramped back room—that's where my approach to training was born.

Not from weight-loss formulas. Not from celebrity routines.

From learning how to guide someone back to their own reflection with a little more kindness.

Not the "new you." Not the "fantasy."

Just the strong, vibrant, you-shaped version that had been there the whole time.

And behind every lesson? The woman who taught them.

Chapter 2: Sunny Side Up

Brooklyn-Born, Bullshit-Resistant, and the Toughest
Overseer I've Ever Had

*Sunny (right) with her sister Gloria, Flatbush, Brooklyn,
around 1930. Already practicing that half-grin that said
she'd get the last word—and usually did.*

Shirley from Flatbush

Before there was me—the trainer, the truth-teller, the
woman who's helped more people get off the floor without
grunting than a team of orthopedic surgeons—there was
Sunny. Born Shirley Wolff. Raised in Flatbush, Brooklyn.
Christmas Eve, 1924.

She got the nickname Sunny because, back then, everyone swore she had a "sunny disposition." Bright. Cheerful. Easy to love.
We laugh about that now.

Because Sunny's disposition? Think storm cloud with a well-timed lightning strike. She's sharp. Sarcastic. Never one to sugarcoat—unless we're talking about the frosting on her birthday cake.

Yes, she's alive. Sharp as ever. And she can still give me a look and toss out a comment that has me feeling six again—reacting, rolling my eyes, caught in that old mother-daughter dance anyone with a mom knows too well.

Sunny is… a lot of things. She's the original no-nonsense blueprint—cut from sarcasm, stitched with sass, and allergic to anything fake. Especially the polite, passive-aggressive vibe of the DC suburbs.

She doesn't soften with age.
Brooklyn runs through her like steel.

Quick with a comeback. Hard to impress. Entirely immune to "baloney".

And it's not some glossy Brooklyn either.
It's loud neighborhoods. Crowded sidewalks. The scent of garlic, onions, carrots, and celery—chicken soup in the making—floating through the walls, mingling with the steam from boiling potatoes and the tang of vinegar from cabbage cooking down in another apartment.

A borough built on immigrants, hustle, and resilience—not trust funds or TikTok.

Sunny grew up bouncing from apartment to apartment—not for adventure, but because rent was a battle her father kept losing. Sometimes they left in the middle of the night. No goodbyes. Just bags packed and lights off. Not her proudest memories. But it was survival, Brooklyn-style.

Fourth-floor walk-ups. Elevators? Forget it—except for one rare building. Otherwise, it was all stairs and breathlessness. Most buildings had dumbwaiters—metal shafts with pulley doors, like vertical mini-elevators for groceries and trash. Quaint now. Back then? Rodent superhighways.
You sent garbage down and prayed nothing came back up.

It wasn't glamorous. But it worked. And for Sunny, that was just life in a city that didn't coddle you.

Phones weren't personal. They were public events.
If someone called, the owner of the candy store or ice cream shop downstairs would lean out and yell, "Shirley! Phone!" And she'd come tearing down in her hand-me-down shoes, soles taped to keep them together.

Her father lasted longest as a butcher. A solid run in a city where rent was always nipping at your heels.

And her mother?
Anna played cards like it was an Olympic event. Her kitchen table was always surrounded by cousins and neighbors—no wine, no cocktails, just coffee, chain-

smoking, and a never-ending buffet of pickled herring, Danish, soft rolls, pumpernickel, and rye. All served with a side of neighborhood gossip.

The table wasn't for homework. It was for life.
When Sunny and her sister Gloria got home from school, their mother handed them a nickel for ice cream.
There was literally no place for them to sit.

Cigarettes ruled the room. Companies gave out free samples like party favors. You wrote in? They mailed you a carton.
Camels showed up on the doorstep like gifts from the nicotine fairy.

The apartment reeked of smoke—always. Not just when the cards were flying.

The Jergens Commercial

Junior high wasn't Sunny's idea of a good time. She liked that having the last name Wolff meant she always sat in the back row, far enough from the teacher to sneak bites of her bagged lunch—omelet on a kaiser roll—during first period, unwrapping wax paper with the precision of a jewel thief. She said the teacher probably noticed but felt sorry for the kids because it was during the Depression years.

She'd rather have been outside playing handball, chalk dust on her hands, running until her legs burned, instead of sitting through lessons she didn't care about.
Then came the day every kid dreaded: class presentation day.

And then...it was Sunny's turn.

She stood up, smoothed her skirt, and made her way to the front of the room with the calm of someone heading to the gallows—hoping for a loophole on the way.

She took a deep breath, turned to face the class, and for a second, paused—letting a small, mischievous smile flicker across her face.

They had no idea what was coming.

She launched into her talk, something about a news event she'd heard on the family radio. And right in the middle of it, she paused again—this time with the perfect timing of a performer dropping in a commercial break.

"Girls, let's stop a moment and look at our hands," she said, with the calm authority of a radio announcer. "Are your hands dry and flaky? They should be soft and smooth. Take a good look. You should be using Jergens Hand Lotion."

Sunny would crack up telling this story, remembering how the entire class—including the teacher—dropped their eyes to examine their hands like they were checking for a disease.

She'd slipped a commercial into her talk just to see if she could pull it off. And she did.

Her girlfriends were furious afterward.

"Why didn't you tell us you were going to do that? We would've done it too!"

Sunny just shrugged. She wanted to be the first. The one with the nerve to try it.

The teacher gave her a B, and Sunny was pissed.
But if she was going to get a B anyway, she figured she might as well have some fun getting there.
And that was Sunny.

Childhood in Brooklyn was one thing. High school? That was its own proving ground.
If school was a circus, home was its own kind of comedy show—
Especially once Socrates arrived.

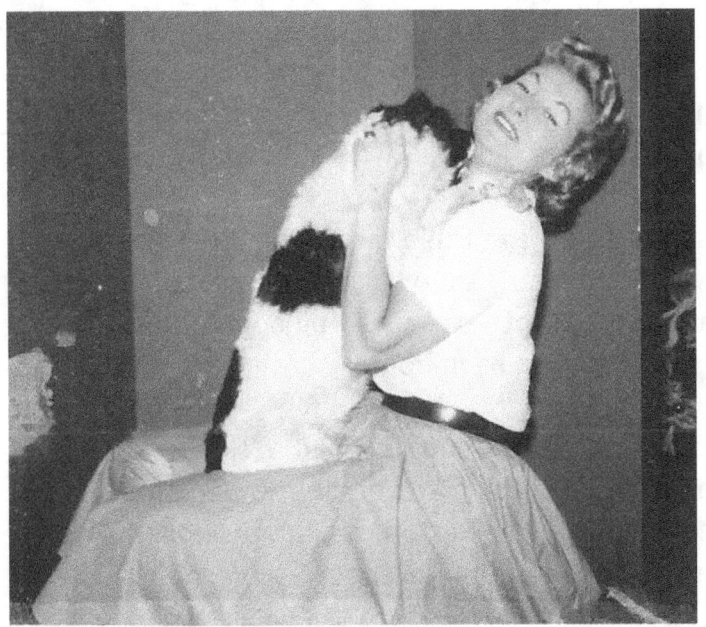

Sunny and Socrates, Brooklyn 1950s. Nobody needed a leash to handle their business.

Socrates and the Elevator Commute

Sunny always said Brooklyn taught her street smarts, but it turns out their dog, Socrates, might've been the real valedictorian.

Her mother, Anna, found Socrates as a trembling puppy under the apartment steps one brutally cold winter morning. One sniff, one soft whimper, and that was it—Socrates was in, for life.

Socrates didn't care where they ended up. Floor didn't matter. Weather didn't matter. And on those rare occasions when the new building came with an elevator, she ignored it—same routine, as if the thing didn't exist.

Rain, snow, or summer haze, Sunny or one of the family would walk her to the elevator. Someone pressed the lobby button, and Socrates trotted in like she owned the building, off to take care of business.

And she didn't waste the opportunity. Socrates was a frisky girl with a fan club—known across the neighborhood for her friendliness with the male dog population and for the litters she brought back home.

When she was ready, she returned to the building, plopped herself in front of the elevator, and waited. Sooner or later, someone pushed the button, the doors opened, and Socrates hopped in—no leash, no escort, no fuss.

Different day, different age. Even the dogs handled their business with a streetwise kind of independence. Everyone knew whose dog was in the elevator—again.

Socrates had her routine down, but Sunny was about to face a different kind of climb—high school in Brooklyn.

And About That High School...

James Madison High School wasn't just any public school. It pumped out legends: Ruth Bader Ginsburg. Bernie Sanders. Elena Kagan. Carole King. Judge Judy. Norm Coleman.

Sunny would remind you—often—just how many presidents, justices, and generational voices walked those same halls.

She may not have made it to the Supreme Court or the Grammy stage, but she showed up every day with style, hustle, and brass buttons before brunch.

Graduation didn't mean settling down. Not for Sunny.

Six Months, Two Spills, and a Side of Free Hamburgers

After high school, Sunny took what little money she had saved and blew down to Miami with her girlfriend Polly. Six months of white sand, coconut trees, and no parents yelling about pins in the bed.

Miami back then wasn't the chaotic sprawl it is today. It was wide open—sun, salt air, and the occasional need to dodge a falling coconut before it turned your beach day into a medical emergency.

They found a cheap room in someone's house, and Sunny needed a job to help cover rent.

Her first gig? A one-shift wonder at a swanky hotel dinner service.

Sunny was athletic, quick, and could dodge a handball like nobody's business—but carrying a loaded food tray in a crowded dining room? That was a different sport.

One wrong step, one slippery moment—and the entire tray launched into orbit. Dinners rained down on tablecloths, hairdos, and lapels like a buffet had exploded. She landed on her backside, sat up, and burst out laughing. Sunny was all over that one.

Fired on the spot. Without pay. For that whopping minute she worked.
Didn't slow her down a second.

Next stop? An ice cream parlor. A local hangout for every army boy in uniform looking for a soda pop and a smile.

Sunny was more than happy to oblige—until day two, when she tried to impress a table of three soldiers.

Young, gorgeous, blonde, with that hourglass figure she never apologized for, Sunny decided to add a little flair. A flash of a smile, a tilt of the head, a sway of the hips. She poured the soda over the ice cream at the table, hoping the fizz and her bright eyes would leave them dazzled.

And boy, did she make an impression.
She missed the glass entirely.

The soda went straight into a soldier's lap, soaking his crisp uniform. He leapt two feet in the air, gasping, arms flailing, cold soda dripping everywhere.

Sunny tried to apologize, once again laughing so hard she couldn't get the words out. Tears streamed down her face.

Sunny wasn't destructive, and she didn't have a mean streak. But as she liked to say, "Shit happens. What are you gonna do after the fact?"

Between shifts and chaos, she and Polly went to USO Centers where soldiers came for rest and rehab. They held dances with live bands, and Sunny had the time of her life. Free hamburgers, soda pop, and men in uniform—who wouldn't show up for that?

They kept the entrance cards and went back again and again, dancing until their feet hurt and laughing until their sides did too.

Eventually, the money ran out. The Miami adventure ended, and Sunny headed back to Brooklyn because her parents needed her to work. Anna had cards to play and Camels to smoke. Charles, who hated being a butcher almost as much as he loved the racetrack, counted on Sunny's paycheck to keep the lights on.

Meanwhile, her younger sister—the "talented one"—got to go to art school, encouraged to pursue her gift while Sunny punched a time clock.

Sunny never complained. But she never really understood it either.

Even now, after everything I know—about her sister's art, about Sunny's quiet genius—I'd argue Sunny was just as talented, if not more so.

Sharp. Fearless. Endlessly observant. With a practical creativity that could solve anything.

She grew up under the weight of someone else's potential. And that kind of burden sticks.

The Racetrack

Sunny's parents, Anna and Charles, loved the racetrack. They'd scoop up every handicap sheet and newspaper clipping they could find, drop them in front of Sunny, and say, "Pick us some winners."

Sunny loved it. She'd spread the papers out, study the odds, and circle her choices for win, place, and show. She picked a few winners. Picked a few losers. But she liked the game— the focus it required. The quiet thrill of being right.

It wasn't the freedom of Miami. But it was a kind of freedom all the same.

Sometimes, she'd go to the track. Sunny wasn't about to bet blind. She'd head down to the paddock to get a look at the horses herself—checking for signs of tampering or injury, seeing if a horse looked off or uncomfortable.

Amazing, considering she'd never been near a horse before. Classic Sunny. Curious. Observant. Determined to figure things out for herself.

And for her—even now, at over a hundred years old—to admit she was good at something? That's saying a lot. She's never been one to brag. Never fully believed in the great qualities she had.

But she was good at this.
Until the day she wasn't.

One afternoon, Sunny was at the track, watching a race, eyes on her picks, when a horse went down mid-race with a broken leg. Someone came out and shot it, right there on the track, in front of everyone.

Sunny ran. Tears streaming. Sick to her stomach.

She never went back.
Never placed another bet.
Never touched another handicap sheet again.

Because for all the toughness she's carried through her life, Sunny's heart has always been stronger than her appetite for a win.

The Math Test She Walked Out Of

Sunny didn't drink. She didn't smoke. Her vice was food.

Chocolate, mostly—anything chocolate that wasn't nailed down. And bread. Crusty rolls. Soft challah. A doughy something tucked inside her handbag for later.

You could stage an intervention at a bakery, and she'd still leave with a bag under her arm.

Food was her comfort, her rebellion, her sedative. And she never apologized for it.

After graduating James Madison in 1943, she skipped college. It was free back then, but she hated school. More importantly, her family needed money. She needed to work.

Her younger sister, Gloria—went on to a famous art school. Sunny bought her supplies. Gloria became a renowned book artist with museum pieces across the country. Sunny got a job. And didn't complain.

School wasn't her thing anyway.

But for a minute, she made a different decision.

She decided—though it wasn't a decision that would last— to apply to Parsons. That Parsons. Manhattan's iconic design school.

She found out when the next entrance test was scheduled, and off she went.

Sunny could draw anything. She was exquisite, even then, with a pencil in her hand. But she especially loved drawing eyes. Maybe because they were small and intense. Maybe because they told a story. Or maybe she figured everyone else would be sketching glamorous gowns, flowing fabric, runway silhouettes— and Sunny, of course, decided to be different.

So, when the entrance test asked for a sketch, she drew an eye. One sharp, unblinking eye, staring straight back from the page.

Then the test hit the math section.

Nope.

It felt too much like high school all over again, and she wanted no part of that. She stood up mid-test, grabbed her handbag (likely with a roll tucked inside), and walked out.

A week later, Parsons called.

They wanted her.

Not for the dress sketches. Not for fashion designs. For the eye.

To this day, Sunny can't figure out what an eye had to do with fashion design.

She never did go. She turned them down.

Later, she admitted that might not have been her finest decision.

Not Enough

Sunny was told from the start she wasn't enough.

Not pretty enough. Not smart enough. Not thin enough. Not rich enough. Over and over, from everyone and everywhere, until those words became her inner soundtrack.

She carried that soundtrack into every room, every mirror, every job she ever took.

The world told her she was too much and not enough, all at once—and it stuck.

And even though she was more than enough, she never felt it. Not for a minute.

I know, because she passed that on to me.

As a young mother, she thought she was doing the right thing—preparing me for a world that would judge me just as harshly. She'd tell me, "I'm doing this for your own good. So, you'll have what I didn't. So, you'll be ready for an unaccepting world."

She meant well. But it felt like war.

Every day was a battle to prove I was enough. To her. To the world. To myself.

My first few decades? They were spent fighting through that mindset, tearing it apart brick by brick, learning where it came from and why it was there in the first place.

Learning to forgive. Learning to grow.

And learning that I am enough, exactly as I am.

Sunny never quite learned that lesson. It was too deeply ingrained. Too heavy to shake off, even in a hundred years.

She carried those doubts with her, whether she realized it or not. But they didn't stop her hands from working or her mind from moving forward.

She and the sewing machine found each other—and it became one of the longest relationships of her life.

Love at First Stitch

She didn't always love sewing.
In junior high, it was part of the curriculum. Nothing elaborate. The assignment was to hand-stitch a single, boring cloth napkin. It was supposed to teach patience, domestic skills, or whatever virtue girls were expected to practice at the time.

Sunny hated it.
She took the napkin home and handed it off to her father, Charles, who actually enjoyed sewing.
She saw no reason not to take advantage of that.

But after high school, everything changed. She discovered the sewing machine.

Back then, department stores like Abraham & Strauss had demo machines right up front—set out for customers to try. A siren song for the curious and the bored.

Sunny would plant herself there during her lunch hour, sometimes for an hour straight, ignoring the salespeople and the side-eyes, teaching herself by feel.

No instructor. No lessons. Just trial, error, and pure stubborn instinct.
Fabric, motion, and a brain that refused to quit until it made something that worked—and looked good doing it.

She didn't need a certificate to tell her she could do it. She just needed a machine, a bit of fabric, and the freedom to figure it out on her own terms.

And it didn't take long before she wasn't just teaching herself.

Other women hovered around those machines—curious but unsure, afraid to touch the buttons or break a needle. Sunny showed them how to wind a bobbin, how to adjust the tension, how to run a straight seam without chewing up the fabric.

She explained the difference between a zigzag and a straight stitch, how to keep the fabric moving, how to fix a jam.

The salespeople didn't mind. They didn't have to do a thing. Sunny became an unpaid demonstrator for Abraham &

Strauss, turning her lunch breaks into free sewing lessons for half of Brooklyn.

She got practice. They got confidence. And the store probably sold a few more machines because of it.

Sunny just considered it a fair trade—and another step in figuring out the life she wanted to stitch together.

She didn't just keep what she learned at home.
Before long, she was ready to take it—and herself—into Manhattan.

Sunny, DC, early 1950s.

Whether she was in the garment district showrooms or posing on the Capitol steps, Sunny knew how to show up— and how to make an impression.

The Showroom Girl

In her twenties, Sunny worked as a showroom girl in Manhattan.
Receptionist. Part-time model. All-purpose front woman for buyers from Jersey.

She lived at home. She wasn't married.
Neither was exactly her preferred lifestyle choice.

But she had a job. A good one.
And the kind of confidence that let her walk into any building in the Garment District and land on her feet.

Still, phones and fittings weren't enough.
When the showroom was quiet, she'd slip into the back—to the factory floor.

She watched the cutters. Studied the pattern makers.
Learned why seams failed, how to adjust a fit, how to reinforce a dart.

No one asked her to. No one taught her.
She taught herself.

Every lull in the day became a lesson—not just in how to sell clothes, but how they were born. What worked. What didn't. And why.

She didn't have a trust fund. Didn't have a degree.
But she had fabric.

Even at the tail end of the Great Depression, when thread
was reused and zippers were sacred, Sunny found scraps
and remnants.

She made her own clothes for work. Looking put together
was part of the job. And she excelled at it. From head to toe.
She may not have had the expense account, but unless you
knew designers, you wouldn't have known the difference.

Garment factories were divided by type: coat district,
blouse district, skirt district. Suits and dresses? Separate
buildings entirely. Sunny worked across them all—one
district, one floor, one skill at a time.

And she brought it all home.

The best cutting surface in the apartment turned out to be
her parents' bed. She'd spread out fabric, lay out patterns,
pin her ideas right into the mattress. And yes, she often
forgot the pins were there—until bedtime.

There were yelps of pain when her parents found them the
hard way. One or the other would come storming into her
room, waving a pin and yelling, while Sunny was stuck
between pulling the covers over her head and trying not to
laugh.

She grinned every time she told that story.

The Marriage She Chose—The Life She Didn't

Somewhere between showroom floors and fabric scraps, she met William—though "love story" might be pushing it.

His name was William. A buyer from Lit Brothers in the showroom. Tall, dark, handsome—and yes, a full head of hair. He proposed in person, holding out a ring balanced on a single rose.

And she said yes.
Because, well... he asked.

They honeymooned in Florida in 1955, and by all accounts, it was exactly what mid-century honeymoons were meant to be: hopeful, humid, and heavily photographed in resort-wear. They drove down in his convertible, and Sunny remembers another detail just as vividly: her mother and the card-playing crew insisted they bring back cartons—dozens—of cigarettes from Florida, where they were cheaper.

Nothing said "marital bliss" like hauling contraband Camels up I-95 for the kitchen-table poker league back in Brooklyn.

After three months of marriage, they moved to the DC Metro area, chasing something that sounded like stability.

But for Sunny, life went from full color to beige.
Her Technicolor dulled. Her Brooklyn vibrancy didn't translate to the quiet cul-de-sacs of suburban Maryland. She became a wife. A mother. But she wasn't happy.

Not in that house. Not in that era. Not in that version of herself.

She did her best.
But she didn't start reinventing herself until her early 50s—when most women were being told to slow down, not start over.

As for William? He wasn't her first choice.
Sunny's one true love was looking for "a girl with money" to help put him through school. He wanted to be an ophthalmologist. The day he called to propose—yes, he called—Sunny told him she was already engaged.
And she meant it.

To this day, she swears that was the real mistake.
Whenever she tells the story, I say, "Well, if you hadn't married Dad, you wouldn't have had me."
She always laughs and replies, "I would have had you no matter who I married."

For the record—I was not adopted.

Built From the Inside Out
(What Sunny Passed Down, and What She Didn't)

Sunny didn't raise me to be soft. She raised me to be sharp.
She taught me the sacred art of the snarky comeback.
The value of telling someone the truth—even if it made them flinch in the fitting room.

If you sell a swimsuit, you better mean it when you say it looks good. And if it looks like crap? You take it off and find something better. No lies. No ego strokes. Just style and honesty.

We traveled together to the New York buying markets like a two-woman hurricane.
Swimsuits, coffee, sarcasm, and sales reps who never saw us coming.

We tore through showrooms, laughed until we cried, and picked the perfect cuts for women who just wanted to feel okay in their own skin.
Those trips? Bootcamp.

She gave me my taste for New York: the pace, the grit, the don't-look-away honesty.
It seeped into my bloodstream.

I stayed in DC. I built my personal training business here.
But every part of my method—the sharpness, the straight talk, the refusal to sell anyone a lie—that came from Sunny.

And yet, it didn't start that smoothly.
She didn't train me. Not really.

At first, I was embarrassed by her no-filter delivery. People were often caught off guard by it.
Her bluntness was like a splash of cold water you didn't see coming. It cleared the air whether you were ready or not.
And she didn't care if you were ready.

She spoke her mind anyway. Loudly. Unapologetically.
Usually while holding up a swimsuit and telling you exactly what worked—and what didn't.

But over time, I found my own voice.
Still direct—but different.
Straightforward with a side of diplomacy.

I do believe I was born—maybe forged—with empathy. A coping mechanism? A need to please? Something deeper?

And there's something I don't share often. But it matters here, because it shaped the trainer—and the person—I became.

Between ages 13 and 18, I dated four boys—young men, really.
All four died in car accidents. While I was dating them.

I wasn't in the cars. I wasn't part of the accidents.
But I was left behind. Every time.

My parents didn't believe in therapy. They didn't let me talk about it.
So, I didn't.

I carried the grief like weight under my skin.
And somewhere in that silence, I developed a permanent sense of urgency. A depth. A seriousness.

Banter, small talk, trivial pursuits? They stopped meaning anything.
My world changed. And with it, so did I.

I became more intense. More complicated.

Harder for some people to deal with. But real. Deep. Honest.

I developed a gut-level belief in the value of life—life that can disappear in a heartbeat.

While Sunny gave me steel, sarcasm, and the power of a good "take it off," the grief carved something else into me.

A soul that refuses to waste time.
A loyalty to truth.
A tolerance for pain—mine and other people's.
And a deep respect for the clients I would one day train.

Their injuries. Their trauma. Their real, lived bodies.

Don't get me wrong—I would give anything for those deaths not to have happened. But they did. And they made me who I am. Just like Sunny did.

One gave me armor.
The other gave me depth.
And together, they made me damn strong.

The Original No-BS Blueprint

Sunny didn't need structured workouts.
She had factory floors, fourth-floor walk-ups, and the cracked sidewalks of Brooklyn.

Real movement. Real sweat.
No stretch breaks. No complaints.

She played ball in the alleys, ran bases between parked cars, swung a broom handle like it was a Louisville Slugger.

The brick walls were her backstop.
The curbs, her dugout.
The boys on the block? Her teammates—when she let them.

Back then, the pavement was the gym, and your shoes were the gear.

Soles wore down fast. You felt every pebble, every shard of glass, every hidden pothole underfoot.
You learned to watch where you stepped.
But you kept moving anyway.

Sunny, late teens, early 1940s.
No gym. No gear. Just a backyard, a pair of sturdy shoes,
and zero excuses.

In public schools back then?
They had real swimming pools. Indoor, tile-lined, built near
the water—because when a lake is near and the ocean
wasn't far, swimming wasn't optional.

Sunny didn't need lessons. She was born to it.
But her girlfriends couldn't swim, so she faked it—stayed in
the beginner class just to stick by their side. Bobbing along
in the shallow end, pretending she couldn't float, kicking
just enough to pass, while she watched out for them.

Then came the Cold War—not the one with missiles and
mushroom clouds, the one with slammed doors and silent
dinners. My parents wrote their own playbook for that war,
and every page was ugly. If you want to know why I read a
room before I ever open my mouth, start there.

No Safe Corners

My father was from Philadelphia.
Their marriage? A battleground.

No Hollywood glow. No slow-dancing in the kitchen. No
safe place to stand.
Just grit and screaming matches that rattled the walls.
Arguments so loud you could feel them in your teeth.
The kind of fights that make a kid want to disappear—or try
to fix what can't be fixed.

There were no safe corners in that house.

Sunny used to say, "Women in my day didn't get divorced."
So, they didn't.
They stayed.
Day after day. Year after year.

And when football season rolled around, it only got louder.
Redskins versus Eagles turned the house into a full-contact
sport.

Two TVs. Two rooms.
Burgundy and gold in one, green and silver in the other.
Shouting through the walls like cannons.

Sundays felt like living inside a stadium that never ran out
of fourth quarters.

One strange thing: Sunny could see a play coming before
the ball even snapped.
She'd watch the stance, the huddle, the defense—and call it
out like she had money on the line.
"Watch the slant. Watch it!"
And she'd be right. Every damn time.

She didn't need a playbook.
Just sharp eyes, a fast mouth, and zero hesitation.

What's Left?

Sunny's days aren't on pause—they're stitched together, one
bold thread at a time.

While I'm in my office—trying to write, plan the next training block—she's in the next room, iPad set up on its stand in the arm of her recliner, the news murmuring in the background, her crochet hook moving like a drummer's sticks.

She doesn't follow patterns. She creates. Color first, always. Right now, it's lime green, brilliant purple, and a fuchsia so loud it could stop traffic. Next month? Who knows. Her work is vibrant, unapologetic, bright—full of life you can see and touch.

Every so often, a text lights up my phone. Sometimes it's an emoji, sometimes it's a full-on email that reads like she dictated it straight to me just to see if she could pull it off. And she does. She always does.

She's got a Google Home she orders around like it's on payroll.
"What's the weather?"
"What's the capital of Kazakhstan?"
"Play some Ella Fitzgerald."

And the speaker answers back with its little polished tone, like even it knows who's running the room.

She's faster, sharper, more curious than most people half her age—and unlike them, she's got nothing to prove.

And the walker? Basic. Four wheels, a handlebar, and her grit. Every afternoon she gets up, grips it, and moves. Knees complaining. Cartilage long gone. And she moves anyway.

Rolling down the hallway, she'll toss a zinger over her
shoulder if you even think about commenting on her pace.

Sunny didn't raise me to be her.
And I'm not.
I'm softer in some places. Harder in others.

I didn't become who I am by copying her.
I became who I am by navigating her sharp edges.
By absorbing lessons, she didn't even know she was
teaching.
By finding my own way forward.

She survived.
So, I learned to endure.
She barked truth, blunt and raw.
So, I learned to listen closer.
She charged head-first into obstacles.
So, I learned to feel what was on the other side.

She didn't hand me strength.
She handed me friction.
And in the heat of that friction, I found my own fire.

If there's anything you like about me—
the humor, the grit,
the refusal to sugarcoat an excuse,
the willingness to tell the truth even when it stings—
that's her.

Thanks, Sunny.
Now let's keep going.

And if you think that fire stayed in one lane, wait until you see what she built out of a needle, a measuring tape, and a streak of Brooklyn that never quit.

Chapter 3: Sunny Fits All

To understand Sunny's pull, you had to see her in action—guiding hesitant customers through the discomfort of being seen, turning moments of vulnerability into quiet victories.

"Magnetic" isn't quite the word.

It was more like gravitational.

Sunny had a way of drawing you in with calm confidence, steady presence, and a gift for seeing what you couldn't yet see in yourself. She knew when to offer reassurance, when to tell the truth gently, and when to stand back while you took a breath.

She never coaxed anyone into a suit. That wasn't her style.

She told the truth—matter-of-fact, clear, direct. She'd lay out the pros and cons without sugarcoating, explaining why something worked—or didn't.

People listened.

Because she respected their choices without pushing.

And because she was right.

I still do, even now.

Even at her age, I respect her eye and instincts when it comes to what works on a body—including mine.

Some customers came in convinced they'd never find a swimsuit they felt okay in, let alone confident.

And somehow, by the time they left, they had.

Often something they never would've picked for themselves.

That was her energy.

Firm kindness. Honest encouragement. An instinct for what worked—and what helped people feel seen, respected, and ready.

But if you really want to know how she became the woman who outfitted half the DC Metro area in spandex and empathy...

You have to start in the pool.

My Pool

I swam competitively through my entire youth—year-round, no off-season, no mercy.

Winter, spring, summer, and fall.

In the water before sunrise, again after sunset.

Chlorine in my hair, goggle marks etched into my face like a badge.

AAU. High school. Every local team that had lane lines and a coach who could yell louder than pool-deck acoustics should allow.

I wasn't asked. I was expected.

Swimming wasn't encouraged—it was non-negotiable.

Part of the family playbook. Handed down, no discussion.

In hindsight? No regrets.

At the time? Let's just say 5 AM laps in an ice-cold pool felt like punishment for a crime I didn't commit.

The darkness. The slap of cold air on wet skin.

The sound of your own breath as you pushed off the wall, lap after lap, while the rest of the world slept—those mornings broke you down and built you up all at once.

Swimming taught me discipline. Routine. Focus.

It gave me a structure that would later become the spine of my career—first in swimwear retail, then in training.

It also gave Sunny something: a problem to solve.

In 1976, the East Germans showed up to the Olympics wearing what people called "paper suits."

Sleek, high-compression fabric no one had seen before.

They cut through water like scalpels.
Performance spiked. Records shattered.

Suddenly, every serious swimmer wanted one.

And Sunny?

She got her hands on one.

I don't know who she called, bribed, or sweet-talked.

But I remember standing on a starting block, shivering under the lights, wearing one of those new suits—modified, of course.

At the time, competition rules didn't allow women to swim in public unless their suits had an extra fabric panel sewn over the crotch.

Yes, really.

Modesty regulations.

For girls about to launch off blocks, lungs burning, trying not to drown while shaving milliseconds off their time.

Sunny didn't blink.

She fixed it herself.

Needle. Thread. Quick seam. High-tech fabric. Done between the morning news and her next cup of coffee.

I dove in, tore through that pool like hell had broken loose, and shattered records I didn't even know I was chasing. Adrenaline. Compression.

A little maternal badassery.

That moment lit something in her.

She started scouring for Lycra spandex—or anything close.

Not for vanity.

For performance.

For empowerment.

Athletes needed gear that worked.

Girls needed suits that didn't sag, shift, or balloon like parachutes at turn two.

Sunny understood that.

She started sourcing, modifying, and testing.

At first for me.

Then for my teammates.

Word spread.

Suddenly, she was outfitting half the swim clubs in the county.

Then came the boys.

A nightmare to outfit—demand outpaced everything.
Boys tore through suits like tissue paper.

Unless you were already on the national team, finding gear
that held up was nearly impossible.

Sunny changed that.

She started in a 100-square-foot nook in the back of a
running shoe store called Phidippides.

Sewing machine next to the only bathroom, which she
turned into a makeshift dressing room with a cracked
mirror and a hook on the door.

Glamorous? Not even close.

Effective? Always.

She'd travel hundreds of miles to find Lycra—the kind that
hugged without binding, stretched without warping, and
could survive a season in chlorine without turning to mush.

Fitting women was tricky.
Fitting men?
Even trickier.

Many of Sunny's customers were competitive male
swimmers, vacationers, and gay men who discovered that
not only could she fit them perfectly—she had style.
And she had a blast with the gays.

They loved her irreverence, her flair, her refusal to whisper about body parts or settle for boring prints.

She'd source wild patterns and outrageous colors, laying them out like jewels—deciding exactly where to place each print.

Because yes, that flower needs to be centered.
If you catch my drift.

They adored her. She adored them back.

A bond built on humor, trust, and the shared truth that the right suit could change how you felt when you stepped out into the world.

The Washington Post caught wind of what she was doing. Again.

They called, wanting a story.

She sent them a custom men's suit—and just for fun, a matching Lycra swim cap.

Once again, she laughed—just picturing a newsroom full of reporters trying to stretch swim caps over the wrong body parts was enough to bring back the first time and the grin that came with it.

Eventually, she outgrew the nook.
Opened her own 6,500-square-foot beast—part boutique, part therapist's office, part war zone every June.

She couldn't find local factories that could handle the four-way stretch of Lycra.
Machines snapped. Threads puckered. Everyone said no.

So, she partnered with small U.S. manufacturers who were crazy enough to try.

Her shop wasn't just a place to buy a swimsuit.

It was a place to be understood.
To be seen.
To be fitted in a way that honored your body, your style, your life.

And, when necessary—
to be told, gently but firmly—
to step away from the wall of black spandex and try again.

The Capitol East Kiss

Sunny set up shop at swim meets all over the region—lugging racks of suits, duffel bags of goggles and caps, and her fearless, cut-to-the-chase presence onto humid pool decks, year after year.

One of those meets was held at the Capitol East Natatorium in Washington, DC—a no-frills facility in a tough part of town, where the ceilings dripped condensation and the echo of whistles bounced off cinderblock walls through chlorine haze.

The team there was coached by an older woman named Jane, who approached Sunny with a kind of quiet urgency.

Jane explained that her swimmers were all young Black men—most from some of the hardest-hit neighborhoods in the city.

They didn't hug. They didn't trust.

They went to school with guns in their backpacks.

And yet, they showed up. They swam.

Then, looking Sunny in the eye, Jane asked:
"Can you help us? I don't have funding for suits. But these kids—they're here, doing the work."

Sunny didn't blink.
"Of course," she said.

No red tape. No drama. No "let me see what I can do." Just yes. What color suits?

And for years, she did it.

She outfitted the entire team. No invoices. No fanfare.

Sunny would show up with gear, spreading suits and caps across a folding table like it was the most natural thing in the world—because to her, it was.

She didn't talk down. Didn't tiptoe. Didn't flinch at the hard edges or the silence.

And that silence? It didn't last.

Over time, the swimmers came to recognize her. They'd head straight for her table, grinning, joking, asking what wild prints she'd brought this time, trying on goggles in front of the warped mirror she carried in her supply kit.

The tension softened. Laughter started to fill the space between transactions.

One afternoon, one of the toughest kids on the team— shoulders squared, eyes cautious—leaned in, curious. "How do I pay you back for all this?"

Sunny didn't miss a beat.
She pointed to her cheek.
"With a kiss."

He paused.
The pool deck felt like it held its breath.

Then, he leaned in—and kissed her.

The entire deck went silent.

Jane stood frozen. The other swimmers stared, jaws dropped.

But Sunny? She beamed.

She told that story for decades—always with a mix of pride, disbelief, and a glint of tears in her eyes.

Because it was never about the kiss.

It was about the trust.
And that trust?
She earned it the only way she knew how—by showing up,
telling the truth, and giving a damn when it counted.

And just when you thought nothing could top that—
here came leather jackets, heavy boots, and two of the most
unexpected customers the store had ever seen.

Leather, Lycra, and Nerves

One sweltering June afternoon, the store was at capacity—
moms, kids, teens, toddlers, all buzzing in the summer
urgency of swim season.

People were grabbing anything that resembled a suit,
tossing options over their arms, calling out sizes,
determined to get in, get fitted, and get to the pool before
the weekend hit.

We were handing out dressing room numbers like deli
tickets, trying to keep the flow moving while the racks
emptied faster than we could refill them.

The air carried hints of sunscreen and tanning lotions,
mixed with the quiet hum of nerves—first-time swim team
parents hoping they were buying the right gear, teenagers
trying on competition suits, vacationers eyeing the brighter
prints they were too shy to wear but wanted anyway.

Then—everything stopped.

The door swung open.

Two men walked in.

Not dads. Not shoppers. Not small.

Over six feet tall, built like linebackers on their day off.

Leather jackets. Black boots. Beards like hedges.

And the way they stood there, hands buried deep in their jacket pockets, arms stiff, bodies still—like they were gripping guns or at least making sure everyone thought they might be—sent a ripple through the entire store.

Every conversation cut mid-sentence.

A mom with three bikinis draped over her arm backed away from the counter.

Even the toddlers felt it and went silent, eyes wide.

And Sunny?

She didn't flinch.

She didn't ask me to call security.

She didn't slip out the back—which, by the way, she once did when Entertainment Tonight rolled up unannounced for a planned interview.

But this?

Two towering, maybe-packing strangers with stone faces and leather creaking at the seams?

Sunny owned it.

She strutted out from behind the glass block counter—hips swinging like she was heading into a Broadway callback.

She didn't blink.

She didn't soften.

She gave them a head-to-toe once-over and said, loud enough for the entire store to hear:
"Hey boys. What can I help you with? Looking for suits for yourselves, your girlfriends, or your wives?"

The taller one blinked.

The other cracked a smile.

She leaned in and said, "Take me, I'm yours!"

It landed. They both burst out laughing.

Next thing I know, she's got an arm looped through each of theirs, guiding them through the racks like she's giving a VIP tour of the Lycra Hall of Fame.

They spent a good thirty minutes browsing, joking, absolutely not holding up the place.

By the time they left, all three were laughing. One of them gave her a full-on hug. The other promised he'd be back with his girlfriend.

Sunny waved them off like they were old regulars, calling after them:
"Come back when you're ready to get your swimsuit. We've got just your color."

The door shut.

The spell broke.

Moms exhaled. Kids went back to whining. Hangers clattered again, like someone hit the defrost button on the room.

Sunny slid back behind the counter, calm as ever, and looked right at me.

They did come back, too.

Not just once—every summer for a few years, like clockwork. They never did bring their girlfriends or wives, despite that promise. They brought themselves, parking those massive motorcycles right on the sidewalk in front of the store, chrome glinting in the sun while they stomped back inside in leather and denim.

They'd grin when they saw Sunny, handing over the helmets and letting her work her magic, helping them find new suits and soft cotton t-shirts that made them look—and feel—like kings of the beach, not just the road.

They came for the suits, sure. But they really came for Sunny.

"Not a chicken shit today."

Beady Little Eyes

They came for suits. They left with trust. And Sunny always made it look easy—even when it wasn't.

Sometimes it was laughter that softened the room.
Other times, it was instinct.

The kind that kicks in when a man walks through the door looking like trouble.

He was scruffy, graying, and a little lost. Jeans sagging just enough to look tired, shirt untucked, hair doing its own thing, eyes darting like he wasn't quite sure where—or who—he was.

Sunny took one look and clocked it immediately.

She shot me a glance and said under her breath, "I've got this."

Translation: He's shady, and I don't trust him yet. You stay put.

She approached him calmly. Friendly, but alert.

Said he was looking for a suit for his wife.

Which, in retail translation, was usually code for: I don't know what I want, and I don't want to say why I'm really here.

Sunny didn't flinch. Didn't back off. She read him.

"You look familiar," she said, watching his face. "Did your kids swim?"

That's when he snapped.
"My children are still alive!"

Most people would've recoiled. Sunny didn't move.

"That's not what I meant," she replied. And then calmly explained how we got our start fitting swim teams across Montgomery County. Parents came in all the time, usually years after the kids had already aged out.

She locked eyes with him. No fear. No apology. Just fact.

The tension in his shoulders dropped. He shuffled toward the goggle rack.

Sunny followed.
"You've got these beady little eyes—try a few on."

That cracked the ice.

She talked him through every pair—strap tension, nose bridge, seal quality. Before long, he was asking questions, cracking jokes, complaining about the price of a $5 kickboard like it was gold-plated.

He left with a bag full of gear.

And just before the door swung closed, he turned back and said,
"This store is probably one of the best-kept secrets in Washington."

Sunny nodded. Then turned to me and deadpanned:
"You know who that was? He anchors Nightline."

She gave me a look that said, And you thought I was gonna let you handle him? Please.

Handled. Sunny-style.

Retail Goggles & Madness

You want to test a woman's patience? Forget bootcamp.
Work a goggle wall in June.

We didn't just sell suits. We sold everything pool-adjacent:
caps, clips, boards, towels, t-shirts, and tics of madness.

But goggles? Goggles were a special brand of hell.

Dozens of styles. Prescription and not. Kid and adult.
Silicone, rubber, no backing.
Three dollars to thirty-five.

People would walk in and want to "try on" every pair. For an hour.

Help with the strap. Help with the seal. Help with the magic pair that didn't leak, fog, or mess up their hair.

"Which one won't leave marks on my face?"
"Which one won't fog up?"
"Which one won't rip out my child's will to live?"

As if we were goggle whisperers.

And after an hour of trying, testing, and fiddling—they'd leave with the $3 pair.

And then bring it back.

"These leaked."

No shit.

They'd hold it up like they were returning a failed parachute.

We'd explain—gently (okay, not always gently)—that goggles weren't indestructible. They weren't waterproof miracles. They were cheap plastic that sat in chlorine. They cracked. They fogged. That's physics.

But customers wanted NASA-level performance for a sandwich-sized budget.

Holding back sarcasm took strength. Smiling? That took the last of Sunny's sanity—what was left of it after 30 years of retail.

People thought we were just a swimsuit shop.

But behind that goggle wall, we were part lifeguard, part therapist, part magician.

And no, goggles didn't pay in sanity. Or commission.

But damn if they didn't give us stories.

Entertainment Tonight & the Chicken Shit Exit

Now seems like a good time to talk about chickens. Specifically, the chicken shit kind.

Because for all her strength, sass, and swagger?
Sunny had one weak spot: television.

We had a longtime customer, wife of a sitting senator, who came in for lap swimsuits. Basic, functional, discreet. No frills.

Then her husband got elected to a higher office.

Entertainment Tonight got wind of it—and us.

They called. Wanted to film a segment.

Sunny took the call. Played it up. Brooklyn charm on full blast. She gave them the green light.

Next week, they showed up. Cameras, clipboard, blowouts.

Sunny took one look out the window, turned to me, and said:
"Char, I'm outta here."

And she was.

Bolted out the back like a pearl-wearing fugitive.

I was stunned.

Left me standing solo under TV lights, trying to explain what kind of suits a senator's wife bought—without saying "tits" on national television.

The camera guy mouthed it at me anyway.

I cracked up.

We got through it. Somehow.

The segment aired. One minute.

A full day of sweating and retakes—for sixty seconds of airtime.

Sunny watched from home, smug and relaxed.
"See?" she said. "That wasn't so bad."

I wanted to strangle her.

But I got it.

That was Sunny. Strong until she bolted. Supportive until she vanished.

But here's the truth:

She gave me the bones. The grit. The foundation.

I learned empathy in contrast to her—not because she spoon-fed it.

She didn't lead with warmth. She led with action.

And when people came in looking for my soft approach, my careful tone, my measured words?
They had no idea that underneath it all—was Sunny.

She taught me to hold ground, not cow-tow (as she said with a wrist flick).

She didn't hand me her lessons.
She forged them through fire.

She gave me a platform. I laid the carpet.

We're different. Always were.

But she's the reason I stand how I stand.

She's the woman behind the suits.
And behind this trainer.

I learned by watching. Then doing.
And in the end, by becoming.

Chapter 4: Fluorescent Truths

It wasn't a gym. But it was a transformation chamber. A place of decisions, doubts, and tiny victories—built under bright lights and lined with mirrors that didn't lie, no matter how badly some customers wanted them to.

That dressing room taught me more about bodies and insecurities than any certification course or anatomy textbook ever could.

Want to know the truth about the human condition? Stick someone under fluorescent lights and hand them a Lycra one-piece. Every unresolved body issue they've ever had will surface faster than you can say "shelf bra."

If you really want to learn about the human body, skip the diagrams. Forget the lecture halls, the bone-colored charts with Latin labels no one remembers, and the professors droning on about muscle insertions.

Just spend a few years in a warm, humming shop filled with the faint scent of new fabric, helping living, breathing, squirming humans inch into unforgiving spandex.

You'll see it all.

What shifts. What sags. What pinches. What someone will go to war over just to hide a stretch mark or a belly fold. What they'll forgive themselves for—and what they won't.

That's where the education happens. Raw. Reluctant. Unedited.

In that dressing room, the truth has nowhere to hide.

Young bodies, figuring themselves out. Old bodies, making peace with the mirror.

Bodies in all shapes and stages—overweight, underweight, long-torso, short-waisted, and everything the mirror doesn't always name.

Some recovering. Some not.

Some worn down by years in an office chair, others carved by a lifetime on the field or in the pool.

They came in with a shape and a story—rarely the same shape as the story told.

And each one, in their own way, stepped into that fitting room, ready or not, hoping to find something that fit.

The conversations started with swimsuits, but they didn't stay there for long.

I'd stand just outside the curtain—alert, listening, reading the pauses between grunts and sighs.

If I heard fumbling, frustration, or that heavy silence that meant defeat, I'd call out, plain as ever:
"Need a hand?"

I never pushed. Never hovered. But I wasn't about to let someone wrestle Lycra alone if they didn't have to.

That's when the truth usually came out.

A trip they were dreading. A body they didn't recognize. A shape they hadn't asked for but now had to dress.

That's when I'd say what I became known for:
"Take it off—we'll find something better."

No fluff. No soft lighting. No false compliments.

Just honesty, and a promise to get them into something that actually fit.

They thought they were coming in for Lycra. And technically, they were.

But underneath all the talk about coverage, support, and "problem areas," what they really wanted was a win.

A suit that didn't make them feel like giving up.

Something that wouldn't betray them in the mirror or make them wish they'd canceled the whole trip.

Something that let them walk out on that beach, into that pool, or onto that boat without a second thought.

If I could help them find that? I was all in.

Not because I believed every suit was magic.

But because I've seen what the wrong one can do.

And how long it lingers.

Just Looking—and Other Lies Women Tell Themselves in Lycra

She walks in—anywhere from age fourteen to eighty-four—eyes darting, shoulders hunched, already half-regretting the decision to leave the house. She's been psyching herself up for days. Maybe weeks. She's heard we know what we're doing. That we can find a suit for any single body. But she's not ready to hear the truth just yet.

I greet her gently, like I'm handling a newborn kitten. Or a live grenade.
"Hi there. Can I help you find something?"

And right on cue, she hits me with the national anthem of swimsuit shopping:
"Oh no, I'm just looking."

Uh-huh. Sure, you are.

Just looking—for what? An escape route?

Because what that really means is: Please don't talk to me. Please don't look at me. Please don't see me. I'm hoping if I hover near this rack of black one-pieces long enough, I'll disappear into the lining.

But I've done this long enough to know silence is only temporary.

Eventually, the questions come.
"Do these run small?"
"Do you have anything with a skirt?"
"Is this going to... hold me in?"

That last one is code for: Can this piece of synthetic fabric erase my body issues, my last decade of stress, and the five pounds of regret I brought back from Cabo?

But the real trouble starts when they grab the wrong size. Every. Single. Time. And it's never too big. Oh no. It's always the size they wish they were. The size they used to be. The size of those favorite jeans from 2003 that haven't buttoned since Obama's first term.

I see them pulling size 10s when they need a 14. I step in, as kindly as possible, and explain:
"Swimwear sizing is different. A size 10 in dresses is probably a 14—or a large—in swimsuits."

Cue the drama.
"Don't tell me what size I wear!"
"I've worn a 10 for years!"

Here's the truth I tried—tried—to gently explain over and over: Just because someone can squeeze into a swimsuit doesn't mean it fits.

Lycra doesn't lie. It stretches, yes. But it doesn't forgive. Push it too far, and the fibers silently scream until they snap. And once they're stretched past their limit? They don't bounce back. Kind of like my patience.

Want an image? Picture a rubber band sitting on your desk—stretch, snap, twist, pull, again and again. After a while, it's limp, useless, and oddly sticky. That's what a too-small swimsuit turns into after two wears. Congratulations.

And the best part? When the customer comes back.
"Oh, this suit was defective. Look at this."

She holds it up like Exhibit A in the courtroom of denial. The fabric's shot. The elastic's dead. Sometimes there's even a hole—dead center in the ass.

One woman tried to claim she bought it that way.

I blinked.
"You bought it with a hole in the back?"
"Yes."
"I was here when you tried it on. I suggested a larger size."

She crossed her arms.
"Well, I bought it like this."

What was I supposed to do—call in a forensic Lycra analyst?

But I didn't fight. Not in front of a packed store. Not when I knew the truth wouldn't matter.

Because it was never just about the suit.

It was about ego. About fantasy. About squeezing into something two sizes too small—just to say you could.

Logic? Please. I've watched perfectly rational women fall to pieces in a swimsuit dressing room because the tag said "Large." Not because it looked bad. Not because it didn't flatter. But because that little woven tag dared to call them what they couldn't admit to themselves.

I spent years trying to convince women it wasn't about the number. It was about the fit.

A well-fitted suit is like a good therapist—it lifts you up, holds you together, and doesn't reveal too much in public.

But too often, the ego won. They'd choose the fantasy over the fit. And when reality set in, they'd blame the Lycra.

All I could do was keep my cool, keep the rubber band analogy ready, and hold out hope for the day society finally stopped equating self-worth with spandex size tags.

I didn't just fit people for swimsuits. I read them.

Observation, conversation, interpretation, and the quiet art of listening—those were my tools long before I ever picked up a clipboard.

Insecurities. Vulnerabilities. The stories people told themselves in the mirror, stitched into posture and breath, hidden in the way a strap was adjusted or arms crossed tight across the chest.

Most came looking for Lycra but left with something else entirely—a reminder they were still strong, still worthy, still capable, even if they couldn't see it at first.

Here's the truth: This was training. Not just the muscle groups, but the whole person—the body as a sum of its parts, plus the psyche holding it all together.

Every fitting became a masterclass in human behavior. Every conversation, a lesson in building trust.

Every small victory—finding the suit that let someone stand taller—a reminder that change starts with feeling seen.

I didn't know it then, but this was the foundation of the trainer I would become.

And when a customer left in a suit that fit, it wasn't just fabric they were wearing.

They walked out carrying themselves differently.

And so, did I.

Chapter 5: Bodies, Armor & the Art of Fit

Hundreds of suits. Thousands of stories. It started out as retail—hangers clattering, receipts jamming in the register, breakroom coffee thick enough to strip paint. But somewhere between the dressing rooms and the deep exhales, it turned into therapy. One swimsuit at a time.

Women came in carrying bags and baggage: tears, panic, silent dread, tightly packed rage. The triggers? Thighs. Boobs. Bellies. Underarms. Sometimes all of the above, depending on the day and the mirror.

Because what stared back at them wasn't just a body. It was a battlefield.

And I became the unlikely field medic—armed with Lycra, a tape measure, and a straight forward, manner.

Sure, we saw men. Teens. Kids squirming in sun shirts and boxy trunks while their parents argued over SPF levels.

But the women? They carried the real weight. Not just on their hips—but in their eyes.

They didn't come in light. They came in for all kinds of reasons—a cruise they were guilted into, a new lap-swimming habit born out of bad knees, a destination wedding in Aruba where they'd rather be a beach towel than a guest.

Some came because their doctor told them to. Some because their daughter insisted. Some just needed a break from the version of themselves they were sick of seeing in every mirror.

But the common thread? Hesitation. Dread. That flicker of panic in the eyes that said: Please let this be less awful than I think it's going to be.

And most of the time? We had the suit.

We carried everything.

Thong bikinis for the bold. Full-coverage suits built like small fortresses—shelf bras, underwire, compression panels, double linings tough enough to rein in a small army.

Mastectomy suits with soft pockets that held space with dignity.

Skirted suits that swished modestly over thighs.

Suits with sleeves for those waging quiet wars against upper arms.

Suits for short torsos, long torsos, and torsos lost somewhere along the way.

You name the insecurity—we had a rack for it.

Some women were lovely. Honest. Raw. Nervous but willing.

They'd walk in bracing for judgment and leave surprised— maybe, just maybe—they didn't deserve it.

With a little nudging, we could ease them out of the funeral-wear section of solid black and into something with life in it.

A raspberry two-piece. A cobalt tank with a neckline that didn't apologize.

They'd step out of the dressing room holding their breath, tugging at the hem, eyes darting for a verdict.
"What do you think?"
"I think," I'd say, "you've got great legs, and you're wasting them under all that Lycra ruffle."

They'd laugh. Sometimes cry. Sometimes both.

And more often than not? They'd buy.

Not just the suit—but the idea that they were still allowed to feel good.

But let's not pretend it was all grace and gratitude.

Some women came in like hurricanes—wrecking racks, hogging stalls, treating us like their personal emotional support team and unpaid private stylist.

One woman came in so many times we practically had her scent etched into the carpet.

Dozens of suits. Hours at a time. Dressing room piles that looked like a clearance bin had exploded.

Every visit came with a monologue: the tragic thighs, the cruel mirrors, the unjust sizing, the endless search for the suit that would finally make her like herself.

And we tried. We really did.

But on her final visit, after another tornado of Lycra left in her wake, my mother—calm as the eye of the storm—pointed to the exit and said:
"That's our door. You know how to use it. Do not come back."

Still the best exit line in swimwear retail history.

Then there was the woman doing jumping jacks behind the curtain—seriously—bouncing like she was testing trampoline durability in Lycra.

"Is anything moving?" she shouted.

I peeked around the edge, assessing the structural integrity.
"Nothing's moving," I said.
"Good," she replied. "I just spent $28,000 on this body."

Then, with the confidence of someone who'd just passed a stress test in spandex, she added:
"I'll take all four suits."

Wonders never cease. Especially when they come with a surgical receipt.

The men? A different breed altogether.

There was always one—sunburned, overconfident, standing at the counter holding a microscopic bikini top like a trophy.
"My girlfriend used to wear this. Now she's gained weight. What do you have for her?"

He'd toss it down like evidence in a domestic lawsuit.

Then—without missing a beat—he'd yank at his own waistband, puff out his chest, and grin:
"Still the same size I wore in college."

Sure, you are, champ. Just ignore the four inches of gut slumping over your belt like a busted pool float.

Reality had clearly left the building. But his ego? Still doing backflips.

We didn't sell illusions. We sold swimsuits.

Fabric, elastic, and hope—stitched together and priced accordingly.

But the line between coverage and confidence? Between reality and the fantasy someone dragged in with them from twenty pounds and fifteen years ago?

Blurry as hell.

Sometimes they left with the suit.

Sometimes they left with a story.

And more often than not, they left with both.

But only one of them actually fit.

And not all the moments were funny.

Some were infuriating.

One of the worst—and far too common—scenes? The mother-daughter ambush.

A woman would barrel into the store, dragging her daughter behind her like checked luggage, and announce— loud enough to rattle the sunglass rack:
"My daughter has these large breasts now, and we need something to hide or contain them. What do you have?"

The daughter—usually a self-conscious teen, sometimes a mortified pre-teen—would turn beet red, eyes darting for the nearest exit.

And then came the gesture.

The mother would lift her arms and demonstrate the "problem"—cupping invisible cantaloupes in the air a foot from her chest, like she was performing some tragic mime act nobody asked for.

Every time, I could feel the heat rise in me.

The tone. The volume. The total disregard for the girl standing right there.

It wasn't just inconsiderate.

It was selfish. Thoughtless. Embarrassing.

A complete blind spot disguised as concern.

And the daughter? You could watch her self-worth shrink in real time.

Another girl made to feel like her body was a problem to be fixed.

Right there, between the cover-ups and the chlorine-resistant racks.

We'd step in—fast, steady, practiced.

Redirect the tone. Lower the volume. Get the daughter out of the spotlight and into a fitting room, one-on-one.

No mirrors. No audience. No lectures. Just space to breathe.

I'd talk to her like a person, not a project.

Ask what she liked. What felt good on her body. What color made her feel less like hiding.

The goal wasn't just to find a suit—it was to give her five damn minutes to feel like a human being instead of a walking embarrassment.

Let her breathe. Let her be.

And then, of course, there were the ones who just couldn't take the pressure.

"I'd rather be at my dentist getting a root canal than try on bathing suits," more than one woman told me—zero irony, fully serious.

And honestly? I got it. I absolutely got it.

This wasn't a shopping trip—it was an emotional MRI under brutal honesty.

Every insecurity, every stretch mark, every ounce of self-doubt laid bare in a three-way mirror that didn't know how to lie.

Of course, she'd rather be numb and drooling in a dental chair.

This work was raw. Personal in a way most people don't expect from retail.

Judgment came from every direction—internal, external, generational, cultural.

And the dressing rooms didn't help.

Between the mirrors, the close quarters, and the vulnerability of stripping down under scrutiny, it was enough to send anyone's confidence sprinting for the exit.

But we weren't just spectators.

We were in it with them.

Every fitting. Every awkward adjustment. Every moment when someone saw themselves a little differently.

We saw nerves that made hands shake while adjusting a strap.

Anger that flashed in a glance at the mirror, as if the reflection had betrayed them.

Frustration that boiled over in a sigh when the size they thought would fit didn't.

Anxiety so thick you could feel it in the air, hovering around the racks like a storm cloud.

Silence that said everything words couldn't, as someone stood there, arms folded, deciding if they were worth the effort of trying again.

But there was also laughter.

Relief that softened shoulders.

A moment of ease when someone looked up and realized they didn't have to hide.

And when it worked—when the suit fit and the story shifted, even a little?

That was magic.

But retail has a shelf life.

Even the meaningful kind.

Especially when you're running a year-round swimwear store in a city with actual seasons and a customer base that hibernates from October to May.

Add a recession or two, rising rents, and a parade of last-minute shoppers demanding miracles on markdown?

Let's just say—the spandex wasn't the only thing getting stretched thin.

This wasn't just a job.

It was a crash course in humanity—in insecurity, projection, pride, denial, and survival.

Every day was another chapter in what people carry and how it shows up when they're half-naked and vulnerable.

And when it was over?

I didn't just walk out with retail experience.

I walked out with an education no psych degree could've touched.

And the best-selling item?

It wasn't the black one-piece or the miracle tankini.

It was always the same:

A suit that fit—and someone who actually listened.

Swimwear retail taught me a lot about people.

Not all of it good.

Not all of it worth repeating.

But some of it?

Too ridiculous to forget.

Because if you spend enough years fitting people in Lycra, you see it all.

And some stories?

They don't just deserve to be told.

They demand it.

Chapter 6: Fitting Room Crimes

There's a myth that swimwear retail is all beach vibes and pretty prints.

Let me break it for you: it's a war zone in Lycra.

People don't walk in calm, centered, or ready to accept what the mirror reflects under fluorescent lights.

They come in desperate. Defensive. Sometimes downright unhinged.

And you—the poor soul handing them a size eight when they swear they're a six—become the bullseye.

The stand-in for every swimsuit that's ever betrayed them.

The punching bag for their hopes, their insecurities, their denial.

Yes, I witnessed kindness, courage, gratitude.

But I also watched people unravel over a piece of synthetic fabric they believed might save their summer.

Tantrums. Theft. Entitlement. Full-volume meltdowns in front of the sale rack.

Some stories, you can laugh off.

Others, you carry.

These?

These are the ones that stuck.

1. The Spandex Raider

She was a repeat offender—the kind you could feel before you saw her. The air tightened the moment she entered.

She didn't browse; she raided.

Stormed in like the building was on fire, grabbing suits with the urgency of someone looting before a flood.

Sizes? Styles? Logic? Optional.

I'd approach—because that's what you do in retail when you've still got a sliver of hope—and maybe offer a suggestion.

Rookie mistake.

Cue the eye roll, the sharp inhale, the clipped "I'm fine."

Which, in retail speak, translates to: Back off and die slowly. I've been bitten by friendlier snakes.

We had a blazing yellow sign, eye-level, impossible to miss: Limit 6 Suits in Dressing Room at a Time.

Clear. Bold. Not up for interpretation.

But she'd hoard like we were rationing spandex for the end of days.

And the moment we reminded her of the policy? Instant tantrum.

On a good day, she'd toss us the cold shoulder.

On a bad day, she'd fling armfuls of suits to the floor like a toddler mid-meltdown at Target, then storm out in silence.

We carried suits in every shape and size imaginable—women's, men's, children's, toddlers'.

But you know what we didn't carry?

Emotional maturity in a retail size medium.

2. Dressing Room Detonation

Some customers didn't rage.

They imploded.

You could always spot them—the "I don't need help" brigade. Silent. Steely. Determined.

They'd snatch six suits without a word, seal the dressing room curtain like they were locking down a crime scene, and vanish into their Lycra isolation chamber.

No eye contact. No questions.

Just vibes and denial.

A few minutes later, I'd tap on the frame.
"How's it going in there? Need another size?"

No reply—just a limp tangle of Lycra shoved under the
curtain like a rejected audition outfit.

A muttered "Too small" if you were lucky.

Never on a hanger, of course. Just a twisted, inside-out
mess—stepped on, stretched, stained with makeup, looking
like it barely survived the first round.

And if you dared peek your head in to help?

You'd get the hiss:
"I said I'm fine."

Which in dressing room terms means: Nothing is fine—and
now it's your problem.

I started calling it The Dead Zone.

Look down, and you'd see the casualties—suits stepped on,
stretched into submission, twisted into shapes they were
never meant to take.

Like the suit tried to escape and failed.

A swimsuit graveyard.

Rest in pieces.

3. Nursing Without Boundaries

This isn't about nursing—it's about the women who treated our fitting rooms like a lactation lounge, left chaos behind, and expected us to thank them for it.

One afternoon, a woman marched in with a baby on her hip like she owned the deed to the place.

No hello. No "Is it okay if I use a room?" Not even eye contact.

She bypassed the sales floor, bypassed me, and headed straight for the dressing rooms, six suits in hand.

Before she could yank the curtain closed, I stepped in—polite but firm:
"If you're planning to try on suits, please leave your bra on. Do not remove it. Breastmilk stains and ruins the suits, and we can't sell them in that condition."

She nodded. Smiled. Gave me the "Got it!" face.

And then did exactly what she wanted.

Curtain closed. Policy ignored. Common decency left outside like a soggy diaper.

She stayed a while, trying on suits she had no intention of buying, letting them soak up whatever was leaking, then breezed out empty-handed—baby back on hip, no shame, no nod, nothing.

When I opened that curtain, the battlefield said it all: three to six suits, damp, spotted, stretched, ruined.

Sunny and I had a rule: we only sold merchandise in perfect condition.

We didn't clean up after breastmilk. Or menstrual leaks, either—or yes, that's coming.

People think Lycra survives anything—saltwater, chlorine, teenage lifeguard ego.

But breastmilk? Breastmilk is its kryptonite.

4. Undergarments Optional. Apparently.

We had signs. Big ones.
Please keep your undergarments on when trying on swimwear. For your hygiene and ours.

Posted in every dressing room. Printed on every fitting card.

But apparently, we could've hired a skywriter or a singing telegram and still—people wouldn't listen.

What were we supposed to do? Ask customers,
"Are you currently on your period?"

Check them like TSA before letting them try on a one-piece?

Yeah, right.

We had no legal ground, no backup, and definitely no dressing room bouncer on staff.

So, we trusted people.

And they betrayed that trust with horrifying regularity.

There is nothing like unfolding what looks like a neatly returned suit—tags still dangling—only to discover a bright red Rorschach blot right in the crotch.

That's not dye transfer. That's someone's monthly visitor.

And they didn't just leave one.

Some women left behind three, four stained suits like they hadn't noticed a thing.

Please.

They noticed.

You're standing in a dressing room, trying on a white swimsuit, and you don't notice you're bleeding?

You don't see it when you take it off? When you fold it and hand it back with a breezy, "Didn't work out"?

That's not an accident.

That's a choice.

A choice to be disrespectful.

To us. To the merchandise. To the next person, trusting that what we sell is clean and wearable.

We didn't scrub. We didn't resell. We didn't lie.

If it wasn't pristine, it was trash.

Another loss on the books.

Retail wasn't glamorous. And we had standards.

We weren't there for glitz. We were there to help people feel okay in their own skin.

And that?

That didn't include hidden surprises stitched into the crotch.

5. The Size-Scouting Scammers

Here's a classic move:

Send in your kid to get fitted for the swim team.

You play the polite parent—friendly smile, grateful tone, nodding like you're actually listening.

We take the time.

We measure.

We explain how jammers should fit, why the straps matter, which cuts won't leave your kid's shoulders red and screaming after a two-hour practice.

We guide. We adjust. We check for growth room.

You nod again, pretending to care.

Maybe even toss out a, "We might place a team order soon."

And then you vanish.

No thank you. No follow-up.

Just a tight smile, a "We're still looking," and tire tracks peeling out of the parking lot.

What we found out later?

You never planned to buy a damn thing.

You were using us like a free fitting service—taking our sizing notes, our expertise, our time—and marching it straight to the team coach or some online discounter to save ten bucks.

We weren't retailers anymore.

We were unpaid consultants with a tape measure.

Imagine building a business around service—fitting people properly, guiding them honestly—and realizing you'd become a glorified measuring stick for cheap skates.

Not a store.

A showroom for people who never planned to spend a dime.

And the kicker?

Entire teams were doing this.

Not just a few rogue parents but coordinated scams.

Coaches in on it. Parents high-fiving each other in the parking lot like they'd pulled off a diamond heist instead of dodging a $68 price tag.

Somewhere out there, a mom running a corporation was sipping Chardonnay, slipping the tags she yanked off the suits in the dressing room into her Louis Vuitton, bragging about how she "saved the team money"—while we stood in the store, lights still on, bills still due, holding the tape measure and the insult.

Let's not get it twisted:

We weren't just selling swimsuits.

We were selling our time, our knowledge, our damn expertise.

Every minute we spent sizing up your kid was a minute we could've spent helping a paying customer—someone who respected the work we did and the business we built.

You think you got a deal?

All you really did was steal.

6. The Eternal Try-On Artist

She followed the rules—at first.

Six suits per round. No complaints. Polite, even cheerful. Just another try-on session.

But after the third trip back to the floor and the fourth, "Do you have this in an 8 long, maybe in teal?"—I knew exactly what I was dealing with.

She'd come out of the dressing room half-dressed, balancing on one foot, hanger marks stamped into her skin like retail tattoos, eyes glazed like she was mid-meditation or mid-meltdown—I couldn't tell which.

Two hours.

Then three.

We brought her water. Sunny and I whispered to one another, "Should we offer a snack?"

Hell, we should've brought her a cot.

She kept rotating suits like she was auditioning for a vacation. Slipping in and out of Lycra like it was therapy, not shopping.

And then, the final blow:
"I didn't really like anything. I'll come back."

And she did.

Again.
And again.

I started recognizing her car before I saw her face, that sinking feeling hitting before she even stepped inside.

I had nightmares of her in a palm-print tankini whispering, "Maybe just one more..."
like a ghost refusing to leave.

And let's be clear:

She wasn't the only one.

She may have set the record at three hours, but two-hour marathons were practically a seasonal event.

These women treated trying on swimsuits like a contact sport—and the dressing room was the arena.

And as good as Sunny and I were, it's really hard to stop someone mid-spiral without a straitjacket, a security guard, and a signed affidavit.

By the third visit, Sunny and I were done.

She walked in, and we looked at each other and knew:

No.
Not again. Not today.

She wasn't shopping.

She was escaping something—staving off a spiral with stretch fabric and false hope, using our store as her therapy room, our time as her distraction, our inventory as her lifeboat.

But this was our store.

Our inventory.

Our rules.

And the answer?

A resounding no.

7. Shoplifting in Diamonds

We first noticed it during inventory—suits showing up with two security tags.

Now, I love a good fashion statement as much as the next retail veteran, but I was pretty sure "double-tagged" wasn't the new look in that luxury zip code where the country club dues are six figures and the golf memberships cost more than a mortgage.

Something was off.

And we were about to find out just how calculated it really was.

These weren't damaged items.

They were decoys.

A crew of well-dressed, well-manicured women—thirty-somethings from that zip code, draped in designer bags and entitlement—had been rotating through the store, pretending to browse while slipping suits into oversized totes.

Lycra made it easy. Roll it, ball it, poof—gone. One minute on the rack, the next headed out the door in a $2,000 purse.

And these weren't teenagers with sticky fingers.

These were polished, country-club women.

Diamonds on their fingers. Botox foreheads. Range Rovers idling in the parking lot.

One of them even turned up in a glossy magazine for her charity work.

Isn't that sweet?

We never called the police.

We didn't need to.

When we finally caught them mid-rotation, slipping a suit into a bag while trying to look casual in their tennis whites, we locked eyes and told them to get out—and not come back.

No yelling. No drama.

Just calm, clipped finality.

Politely, of course.

Because retail teaches you how to hold the door open with a smile... while your soul screams into the stockroom.

You learn fast in this business:

The store isn't just where you sell things.

It's where you grow teeth.

And while we eventually built something big enough to scare off the petty thieves and professional hagglers, it didn't start that way.

It started with thread.

A bathroom.

And a woman who saw a swimsuit not just as fabric—but as a way forward.

Selling swimwear by day, building a future out of it by night.

Some people really can do it all.

And if you want to understand how we got there—how we built something that could hold its ground—
you have to start here.

Chapter 7: From Backroom to Full Tilt

The Fast Rise of a Swimwear Original

Before the 6,500-square-foot retail aquarium—with tiled walls and a floor the color of chlorinated dreams—there was a back room.

No storefront. No sign. No foot traffic.
Just a cramped, forgotten storage space stuffed with fabric, patterns, a sewing machine, and the first suits Sunny ever made, hanging in neat rows like secrets.

When a customer needed to try something on, the only private spot left was the bathroom. Shared. Fluorescent-lit. A piece of masking tape slapped to the door: Please Knock.

Sunny built the business the way most underdog stories start—at home.
Bolts of Lycra where the dinner plates should have been. Patterns stacked next to placemats. Thread spools rolling across the floor while the sewing machine talked louder than anyone in the room.

Swimsuits by day. Leftovers by night. Hustle stitched into every seam.

Eventually, she carved out a cramped corner in the back of a local running shoe store—a forgotten room that smelled like cardboard and chalk dust.

Most customers never wandered that far.
Not until they discovered Sunny.

Out front? Beige carpeting and shelves of basic sneakers.
In the back? A needle in constant motion, fabric draped
over every surface like barricades, and a sewing machine so
loud it might as well have been a call to arms.

Her stockroom was a single shelf.
Her table was folding.
Her dressing room was still the bathroom.

Vision, though? That filled every inch of the place.

And it spread.

Word of mouth. Women telling their friends, who told their
sisters, who told their coworkers.
They came in curious and left converted—holding
swimsuits that did what no department store had ever done
for them.

Not just fit.
Flatter. Hold. Lift.
No riding up. No pinching.

The kind of miracle most women didn't even realize they
were allowed to ask for.

Over time, as the shoe store limped toward extinction,
Sunny outlasted it.

When the owners finally shut down, she took over the lease.
No fanfare, no ribbon-cutting—just keys in hand, lights on,
and suddenly, the place was hers.

Next door was Spa Lady, a women-only fitness studio blasting early-'80s beats while an instructor barked, "Tighten those glutes! Summer bodies start now!" into a headset.

Women spilled out, red-faced and ponytailed, and wandered straight into Sunny's shop—still sweaty, still catching their breath—looking for swimsuits that wouldn't betray their body type.

Sunny, being Sunny, saw an opportunity before anyone else did.

She started sourcing from bold, upstart manufacturers who were cranking out leotards—thong leotards—and slick Lycra tights to match.

High-cut. High-shine. Wildly un-DC.

No one else in the area was carrying anything like it.

It was daring. It was smart. It was Sunny—ten steps ahead.

At first, I didn't get it.

The thongs? The shimmer? Cuts so high they belonged on a Vegas stage?
We were in buttoned-up, khaki-washed DC—not Miami Beach.

But Sunny knew momentum when she saw it.

And when I finally tried one on?

I got it.

Confident. Powerful. Just this side of risqué.

We put a display up front. They sold like hotcakes with a side of rebellion.

Sometimes the manager from Spa Lady would burst through our door, panic in her eyes, sweat dripping down her face.
"Can you teach a class? Our instructor flaked."

If I could peel away from a fitting or whatever spandex-stitching crisis was happening, I'd say,
"Absolutely. Give me five minutes."

And just like that, I'd be across the hall leading squats to Maniac in a metallic blue thong leotard.

All in a day's work.

The store kept growing.

We built dressing rooms that looked like hula huts—bamboo siding, raffia roofs, a little slice of island fantasy tucked inside a Rockville strip mall.

The rent was low. The space was manageable.

And the business was booming.

Looking back, we probably should have stayed put.

But ambition has a price. When the buzz builds, and the demand gets loud, it's easy to believe that more space will fix the chaos the last step created.

Bigger leases. Higher taxes. Landlords waiting to cash in.

And so, we jumped.

6,500 square feet. Full-on indoor pool vibes.

Traffic doubled, then tripled. So did the hours, the stress, and the taxes.

Sunny's sewing machine went home.
The volume was too high, the margins too tight, and nobody had time for free alterations anymore.

Those early days, though? They were gritty. Resourceful.

Pure Sunny.

I look back on that era—and think:
How the hell did I do it?

But this line of work doesn't slow down.

Just when you think you've seen it all, the universe—or some rep from L.A.—throws a curveball your way.

And sometimes, that curveball doesn't come from a fitting room or a showroom.

It comes from a microphone.

And that's how a couple of women who could barely catch their breath between fittings ended up live on the radio, with a microphone daring us to keep up.

Chapter 8: On Air, Off Guard

You'd think advertising a swimwear store would be simple:
Buy a block in The Washingtonian, run a few print ads in
The Post, and let the suits sell themselves.

But Sunny was never one to leave things to chance—
or to silence.

We had this customer, a local radio host with a weekday
morning talk show that half the DC Metro seemed to listen
to while stuck on the Beltway.
Great guy. Outgoing, loud in the best way.

His entire family came in for suits, and Sunny, of course,
worked the fitting room like a cocktail party—cracking
jokes, tossing one-liners, building rapport until it was
impossible not to like her.
Or to leave without a new suit.

Before long, we were advertising during his time slot.

Then came the invitation:
"Come to the station. Tape the ads yourselves. Use your
voices."

You think, Great, I'll read a 30-second script and we're out
the door before lunch.
Yeah.
No.

Turns out, reading a script into a microphone while a
producer stares at you through a glass window is not the

same as telling someone how to fit a swimsuit in a dressing room.
The inflection, the pacing, the "smile in your voice" they want—getting it all to sound natural while a clock is ticking?
Nightmare fuel.

I must have done a dozen takes—each one falling flat or too stiff or too fast or too slow—until an hour later, we finally had thirty seconds they were willing to air.

And then, within a month, the producer decided it would be fun to have us live on air.

Live.
Not rehearsed, not pre-recorded, not safe.

Here's something most people don't know about me:
I'm an introvert.

Yep, even now.
I can do one-on-one, no problem. I can hold my ground and speak my mind.
But I hate small talk, and I'll avoid standing in front of a crowd if I can help it.

Being on radio—even sight unseen—still felt like standing under a spotlight without a script.
Words stumble, the mouth goes dry, and somehow your brain picks the worst possible moment to short-circuit.

Sunny?
Different story.

She thrived on it.

It was pouring that morning, cold despite being mid-summer, and the host opened with:
"Today we have Sunny and Char with us to talk about their swimwear shop."

Sunny didn't miss a beat.
"Don't you think it would be more appropriate if we discussed umbrellas and ponchos this morning?"

She had them laughing before the second question.

They asked about the suits we carried, how we helped women find the right fit.
Eventually, they turned to me, hoping to pull me into the conversation:

"So, Char, do you have a style you like to wear?"

I could feel my face turn three shades of red—fortunately for me, invisible to the audience, but clear as daylight to everyone in the studio.

"Oh, I see you blushing! I'll take that as you like to wear those little bikinis we see in your shop? How about those sideless wonders we've heard all about?"

I mumbled something worthless, wishing I could crawl under the console.
Here I was, with posters of me wearing suits all over the store, never giving a damn what people thought—and yet, live on radio, I was a puddle.

Sunny took over.
Naturally.

We were invited back a second time to talk about this brand
we carried called Miracle Suits—suits designed to
compress, lift, smooth, and generally make a woman's
figure look its best, even if she wasn't feeling her best.
Some even had built-in butt pads for a little extra lift where
nature hadn't provided.

When they asked Sunny about the Miracle Suit, she didn't
miss her chance.
"Sure, we carry the Miracle Suit," she said, "as long as
you're not expecting it to win the lottery for you."

Or any other kind of miracle, for that matter.

That was Sunny—honest, funny, and always ready to handle
the room, even if the room was an entire radio audience.

And me?
I eventually found my voice.
But let's just say... it took a few Miracle Suits' worth of
support to get there.

And speaking of improbable support—

Chapter 9: The Sideless Summer

For a couple of hot, fast-moving months, we sold sideless swimsuits—one- and two-piece.
Yes, sideless.

Picture it: two triangles of Lycra—front and back—held together by what looked like a decorative clamp but was really a cleverly engineered wire.
Not painful. Just... improbable.

The bikini version barely counted as coverage.
The one-piece? A one-piece in name only.

Naturally, I wore one.
The bikini, of course.
For two summers.
Because why the hell not?

It was the '80s. It was Lycra. I was tan.
Too tan, as it turns out—I'm paying for it now, slathering SPF like it's holy water.
But back then?

It was fabulous.
Totally unique.
Totally ridiculous.
And completely awesome.

There's a photo floating around somewhere of me in the one-piece version—high-cut, graphic print, sideless to the point of causing traffic accidents.
It wasn't so much a swimsuit as a geometry problem.

We blew up those photos—both the bikini and the one-piece—mounted them on foam board and hung them near the dressing rooms.
Trust me:
They sold suits.

When the rack emptied, the posters came down.
Rotation tight. Strategy solid. Buzz real.

The local papers caught wind of the "sideless suit" sensation, and suddenly we had free press, a line out the door—and plenty of gawkers.

Women with real figures came in—curvy, confident, sometimes nervous, always curious.
And the gay men?
They got it. They knew how to wear it, how to style it, how to own it.

Best kind of customers:
Bold. Fun. Fearless.

Side note—because it always cracked me up:
The men who came in asking for racing-style Speedos but weren't on a team?
Nine times out of ten, they were European.
And usually straight.

The gay men brought flair, color, and cheek.
The Europeans? Just blunt confidence and no patience for American prudery.

It was a riot.
Camp, couture, and a dependable source of revenue.

But Sunny?
After we sold out that first run, she quietly decided not to reorder.
Not because they didn't sell—they flew out the door.
But because of the looks.
The stares.
The parents dragging their kids out like we were running a peep show in a suburban strip mall.

That was our town.
Uptight. Performatively proper.
Where boldness had a two-week shelf life before mall management got a complaint.

Still—for one short, glorious moment—we were the only store in the region slinging sideless Lycra and making people question their morals...
and their tan lines.

And for the record?
I couldn't have cared less what people thought of me in that sideless two-piece—poolside, beachside, wherever.
Let them stare. Let them whisper.
Or, if they had the guts, let them ask me how the damn thing stayed on.
I'd explain it.
Proudly.
In detail.

But the store?

That was different.
We had a core clientele—family-oriented, loyal, PTA
presidents and soccer moms.

We didn't cave.
But we did adapt.
And there's a difference.

We had our moment in the sun—literally and figuratively.
Sideless suits. Fearless customers.
And a store that felt like something we created, not
something we inherited.

But even a runway moment has its limits—
especially in a town where discount culture ruled the day.
Sooner or later, the Lycra had to stretch to fit not just
bodies—
but expectations.
And that's where the real battle began.

Chapter 10: "Full Price? In This Town?"

Why I'd Rather Sell My Soul Than Swimwear in the Land of the Discount

There's a stretch of road that could've doubled as my personal Vietnam.

It started innocently enough in Georgetown—posh, preppy, full of promise.
Then it crept north like a retail virus—through Chevy Chase, Bethesda, Rockville, Gaithersburg... all the way to Frederick.

To the untrained eye, it was just Wisconsin Avenue turning into Rockville Pike, then Frederick Road.
To those of us in the business?
It was the Grand Prix of Discount Hell.

By the late '80s, that corridor had more discounters per square mile than anywhere else in the United States.

Think about that.
Not New York.
Not L.A.
Not Chicago.
Bethesda.

Back in the day, when manufacturers wound up with overstock—wrong dye lot, discontinued fabric, last season's cut—they shipped it overseas and let someone else deal with it.

Then some genius decided, "Why give it away overseas when we can shovel it into our own backyard? Suburban bargain hunters won't know—or care—what season it's from."

And that's how the discounters were born.
Big-box stores, basement outlets, parking-lot pop-ups.
No fit. No service. Just piles of cheap suits for anyone willing to dig.

Buy a thousand mismatched, outdated suits. Slap on a sticker:
"Originally $120 — Now Only $29.99!"

Boom. Sold.
And sometimes? Even less.

Here's the part that still makes me cringe—because it's true:
If it had been me? A slightly off color, close enough fit, and a $90 savings?
Yeah... I might've bought it too.

Meanwhile, we were in the trenches.
Flying to New York and L.A. showrooms.

Hand-picking styles.
Sourcing the newest performance fabrics.
Making sure we had every cut, shape, and solution for every unique body that walked through our door.

We didn't buy in bulk.
We bought with intention.

And we fitted our customers with care—one awkward, exposed body at a time.

But did any of that matter?
Not when Susie Shopper stormed in waving a flyer from Bob's Bikini Basement, claiming she could get "the same suit" for a quarter of the price.

Never mind that it was three years old, sun-faded, and fit like a wet sock.
She demanded we match it.
Demanded.

We weren't a charity.
We weren't a non-profit for the aesthetically insecure.
We were a damn business.

With overhead. Payroll. Inventory. Rent. Light bulbs. And about forty ruined suits a month from people who couldn't keep their underwear on.

But try explaining that to the woman who wanted 20% off because she was buying two suits. Or because she was paying in cash. Or because she promised—promised—to tell her friends to shop here. (They never did.)

And the classic:
"I'll buy it if you knock ten bucks off."
To which I always wanted to respond:
"I'll sell it if you knock ten percent off your attitude."

It got worse.
Some of them came in just to use us.

We'd spend hours fitting them. Hours. Trying different styles. Brands. Sizes. Pulling inventory. Making suggestions. Adjusting straps. Explaining support. Acting like their personal Lycra concierge.

And then—after all that—they'd leave with a smile and a: "Thanks, I'll think about it."
Translation: I just wrote down the brand and size so I can hunt it online or at Bob's Basement for twelve bucks and a hangnail.

And many did.
Some even had the balls to brag about it when they came back.
"Oh, I found the same one for less."
No, you didn't.
You found a knockoff made from recycled shower curtains.
And it fits like betrayal.

That's when I realized:
I was done selling things.
Done with people confusing a discount with a right.
Done being a warm-blooded Yelp review target.
Done shaving off dollars until there was nothing left but lint.

I was never—never—going to sell a retail product again.

No more returns.
No more tag swapping.
No more negotiating with someone who thought being a repeat customer was equivalent to buying a yacht.

What I would sell?
Me.
My skill.
My time.
My instinct.
My spine.

I'd become the product.
And let me tell you:
There would be no negotiating.
No bartering.
No markdowns.
No goddamn thing but me.

I wouldn't be folded and forgotten in a corner.
I wouldn't be two seasons old.
I wouldn't be shoved under a clearance rack while some size-six-in-her-mind demanded a manager.

I was the product now.
And this time?
I came with boundaries.

I walked away from retail bruised, but clear-eyed.
And what I took with me?
Wasn't merchandise.
It was memory.
It was muscle memory.

It was the ability to size someone up—in the best way—and call bullshit with a tape measure in one hand and compassion in the other.

And let's just say—
In the world of personal training?
That skill came in handier than any bikini ever did.

Chapter 11: Lycra Only Does So Much

Lycra, Luncheons & the Longest Necks in Delaware

The world sells "slimming" and "shaping."
I sell real talk—and I've got receipts made of stretch fabric.

Let's talk about Lycra.
Or Spandex. Or Elastane.
Same synthetic circus, different ringmasters.

You've seen the promises: shaping, smoothing, sculpting.
Make no mistake—it's a glorified elastic prison wrapped in
marketing copy.
The original miracle fiber—designed to stretch like your
patience and snap back like your ex's excuses.

Invented in some sterile DuPont lab by people with better
pension plans than you'll ever see, elastane changed
everything.
Especially for women expected to shrink, lift, compress,
and contort themselves into swimwear-sized dignity—
without passing out in the process.

At the Mansion

Sunny and I were once invited to the DuPont estate.
A Delaware mansion so pristine it looked like it had never
heard of dog hair or takeout containers.

Reception and luncheon, they said.
A little thank-you for carrying their sacred Lycra in our
scrappy suburban swimsuit shop.

We arrived dressed respectably.
We left... stunned.

Picture this:
An indoor swimming pool the size of an Olympic ego.
Round tables draped in linen so crisp it probably snapped.
Orchid centerpieces. Napkins folded like swans.
Waitstaff floating by with trays of food so delicate it
practically apologized for existing.

First course? A micro-salad of frisée and baby arugula with
edible gold flakes.
Followed by a tower of lobster medallions stacked like a
Jenga game from Versailles.
Dessert might've been spun sugar shaped like a Fabergé
egg—I wouldn't know.
I was too distracted by the guests.

Everyone looked airbrushed in real life.
The men were straight out of a Rolex ad.
The women? Blonde. Glossy. Coiffed within an inch of their
structural integrity.
They sat with posture that looked surgically installed.

And their necks—
Long, elegant, swanlike.
Hermès scarves wrapped like statements of superiority.
I began to wonder if Delaware had a secret orthopedic
stretching ritual no one else knew about.

Sunny and me?
We didn't belong.

This wasn't showroom chaos or swimwear market madness.
This was Stepford on a platinum platter.

And for once—we didn't even whisper.
No sarcastic side bars. No muttered commentary.
Just silence.
A full-blown no worder.

Then came the models.
A parade of genetically blessed humans gliding around the pool in next season's swimwear.
Suits that whispered promises:
Buy me, and you too can look like this.

Lycra was the star of the show—
stretched over taut abs and perky everything,
held in place by invisible engineering
and the silent screams of millions of average women
who would try one on and immediately question their life choices.

That part?
That was familiar.
Sunny and I would size up a suit like a mechanic sizing up a carburetor.
Fabric. Cut. Function.
If we liked it, we ordered it. If not, we passed.
We weren't dazzled. We weren't jealous. We weren't fooled.

But the guests?
They watched with open mouths like they'd just seen God in a size two.

I didn't envy them. I envied the quiet. The luxury of forgetting that outside those walls, the real work was waiting—and it had my name on it.

When the Seams Split

But eventually, the seams started to split.
On the business. On the industry. On me.

DC changed.
The market got crowded.
The margins disappeared.

And I was done.
Done selling second skins to people who deserved more than a tagline and a tight fit.

So, I stepped out of the dressing room.
And into something even riskier:
Myself.

Welcome to the recession.
Hope you brought a towel.

Chapter 12: Recession Reps

The End of Retail. The Start of Me.

When the economy tanked, so did the store.
But just like in training, you don't stay down.
You pivot. You push. You get back up.
No drama. Just the next move.

Late '80s, early '90s—recession didn't knock.
It screeched across the showroom floor and parked itself in
every register, every receipt, every nervous laugh from a
customer trying to "just look" without buying.

The Gulf War sent oil prices on a joyride, and guess what
Lycra's made of?
Spandex, elastane, Lycra—call it what you want, it's
petroleum's stretchier cousin.
Pulled from crude oil, spun into thread, sewn into hope.

Crude prices nearly doubled.
And so did our headaches.

And when the recession hit?
Those same manufacturers stopped shipping overstock
overseas.
They funneled it right back into our backyard—into every
bargain bin, big-box, and basement discounter they could
find.
Five-dollar suits on every rack. Suits that cost us forty just
to bring through the door.

Meanwhile, fewer people were traveling.

Our year-round revenue lifeline dried up like a final-sale
bikini left in the sun too long.

Those who were traveling had a new strategy:
Come in, get fitted, ask questions, take notes—
then walk out empty-handed to find the same suit at half
the price.

We became the showroom.
Someone else got the sale.

And when that happens enough times, there's only one way
the story ends.

Eventually, we closed.
We found a jobber to take what was left—
boxes of Lycra in loud prints and quiet colors, each one a
reminder:
discount culture doesn't blink, even when you're drowning.

I locked the door for the last time and stood there for a
second, hand still on the key, realizing how much of myself
had been stitched into that place.
The racks thinned.
The register slowed.
And for the first time in years, I had moments of quiet
between customers—
moments that were mine.

And in that quiet, a thought started tapping:
What if I didn't just work to sell something?
What if I worked to become something?

We spend most of our waking lives working.
If you're lucky, you love it.
If you don't, that's a heavy way to live.

At the gym, I started noticing things.
Not just quads and delts but faces.
That glazed-over look you see in people grinding through
another rep while they're really somewhere else.
And I found myself wondering: if none of this—bills, kids,
mortgages—were holding them hostage, would they still
show up to the same job every Monday?
You already know the answer.
Almost every one of them would trade places with
someone—anyone—if it meant feeling alive again.

I was already spending more time at the gym than
anywhere else—lifting, sweating, pushing limits because it
felt right.
And as the store wound down, that gym time became more
than a habit.
It was a clue.

Then one day, a guy from the gym walked in.
Between clearance racks and the last of the Lycra, he made
me an offer that would change everything.

I didn't know it yet, but that conversation was about to
close one chapter and open another.
Next time you see me?
I won't be behind a cash register.

The store closed.
I stepped into something new.

Got certified.
Took the reins.
And didn't look back.

Retail was over.
The next chapter?
Me.

But before I stepped out for good, there was one last thing I had to face: the walls themselves—and everything I'd pinned to them.

Chapter 13: Owning the Image

Posters, Presence, and the Version of Me That Sold the Damn Suits

After the store closed, one thing still hung in my head as much as it had on those walls: the damn posters.

Let's get something straight: those photos?
They weren't just there to pretty up the place.
They were the place.
They told the story before I opened my mouth.

You don't build a business out of Lycra and grit—and keep the lights on month after month—without a little vanity, a lot of nerve, and one unspoken challenge:
Look at me.
Now try this on.

The Photos Were the Marketing

The suits were loud.
So, we got louder.

Manufacturers didn't send posters, polished campaigns, or even all the suits we ordered? Fine.
We became our own marketing team.
I modeled the suits. Sunny took the photos.
We blew them up to poster size, mounted them on foam board, and hung them around the store like our own private Times Square—no tourists, just truth in spandex.

People didn't buy because of some glossy catalog.
They bought because they saw something real—me.

Not a mannequin. Not a filtered fantasy.
Someone walking, laughing, bending to pick up a hanger—
and not disappearing under the overhead glare.

That's not just retail.
That's a visual memoir.

Every suit had a vibe.
Every poster? A moment.
And those moments belong here just as much as the words.

More Than Just Pictures

Maybe.
But let's be clear—I'm not here to impress the TikTok
crowd.
I'm here to tell the truth.

You don't have to be 24, wrapped in a ring light, peddling
powdered collagen, to tell a hell of a story.
Younger readers don't need me to look like them.
They need someone who's been through it.
Who built something from scratch.
Who burned out, came back, and didn't flinch when things
got awkward—or hard—or sweaty.

You want real?
You're looking at it.
Full Technicolor Lycra. No filters. No apologies.

And to the older women—who might glance at those photos
and think, Well, I never looked like that—

I say this with all the Brooklyn-bred love and sass I
inherited from Sunny:

You don't have to.
This isn't about measuring up.
It's about showing up.

In your body.
In your time.
In your story.

If mine helps you own yours a little louder?
Then it's already doing its job.

Taking Them Down

I still have those posters.
I smile every time I see them—ridiculous, fabulous, fearless
foam boards from an era when we simply went for it.
I couldn't toss them if I tried.
They're not about perfection.
They're about presence.

Do I still look like that?
Yes and no.
I'm still me.
But I've grown into my own face.
Sharper here, softer there.
A few well-earned laugh lines.
Hair changes. Makeup becomes more of a chore—though
sometimes, it's still a fun one.

If the photos make you uncomfortable—for whatever
reason—that's okay.
If you don't relate to the hair, the hip cut, the confidence?
Trust me—there were moments I was nervous as hell in
those suits.

Keep reading.
You might surprise yourself.

And if you're one of the ones who thinks I should've toned
it down, played it modest, stayed quiet?
Well. Ask yourself:

Who's being judgmental now?
And who gets to move along?

The posters didn't come down all at once.
They came down as the suits disappeared—one bold cut,
one bright print at a time.
Some customers asked if we'd restock.
Others wanted to buy the foam board with my face on it.

What they didn't see was me—standing there with a staple
remover in one hand and a pit in my stomach.
I wasn't just closing up shop.
I was taking down a version of myself I'd spent years
building.

I didn't know what came next.
But I know now:

Taking those posters down wasn't just about the store.
It was stripping off the version of me that sold the suits—

to make room for the one that wasn't for sale.

Next time?
It wouldn't be foam board.
It'd be flesh and grit.

Chapter 14: The Product Became Me

Retail Taught Me Presence. Training Required All of It.

The store was gone, but the weight of it didn't leave with
the racks.
Shutting it down had stripped me raw—box by box, hanger
by hanger—until the only thing left was a body that still
needed somewhere to put all that fight.

So I went to the only place that made sense.
The gym.

During the final months of shutting down the store,
workouts weren't a luxury.
They were structure.
The steel beam holding up everything else.

Lifting and cardio became non-negotiable.
Not as escape.
As a lifeline.

And when the nerves crept in—when my mind started
running marathons of panic:
How will I pay the mortgage? What about the car? What
comes next? —
I'd drive to the gym.
Grip the bar.
Push through another brutal workout.

Not going wasn't an option.
The gym was the only place where I didn't have to negotiate
with anyone—
not about price,

not about size,
not about what might still be stuck in a freight shipment
somewhere between here and Los Angeles.

There were no markdowns.
No passive-aggressive bargaining.
No haggling over discount codes.
There was the barbell.
The breath.
The next rep.

And that's where the seed took root:

What if the thing that kept me strong... could also keep me
afloat?
Not just physically.
Financially.
Emotionally.

What if I stopped selling a product—
and became the product?

Retail trained me to read people like a crime scene.
The way they step into a room, already braced for impact.
The pause in their voice when they're not sure they belong
there.
The flash in their eyes—the kind that begs for one honest
answer that won't gut them.

Training required all of that—
and more.

Because training wasn't just about squats and sets.

It was about trust.
It was knowing when to push and when to pause.
When to hold someone accountable, and when to let them breathe.

In retail, we were front and center.
Guiding choices.
Reading faces.

In training?
Same setup.
Higher stakes.

Session after session, I'd stand face-to-face with someone's reality—
and my own.

But closing that store?
That was a slow, surgical goodbye.
Box by box.
Rack by rack.
History unhooked from hangers and folded into clearance bins.

It wasn't just a store.
It was the place where I'd learned how to hustle.
How to read people.
How to hold my ground.

And now?
I needed a new map.
A new mission.
One that mattered.

I started asking people—customers, neighbors, gym regulars—anyone who'd talk:
Do you love what you do?
Then I'd hit them with the kicker:
If you won the lottery tomorrow, would you still go to work?

That question always landed like I'd asked them to move to Mongolia and start over as a llama whisperer.
The look?
Part disbelief, part exhaustion.
"No way," they'd say.
"I've got bills... a mortgage... kids..."

I got it.
But I also knew this:
I didn't want a life I had to talk myself into.

I knew what I loved—lifting, training, helping people feel strong.
But I also knew that turning it into a job would change it.

That sacred gym time?
That was mine.
It was where I sorted stress, moved through fear, reclaimed power.

To make it work, I'd have to give some of that up.
And I was willing.

Even knowing that professionalism came with its own wardrobe—

like Lycra so tight it left a seam mark in your soul.

Thong leotards.
Layered socks.
Fitness fashion by way of punishment.

But hey—there were worse uniforms.

Still, I couldn't not do it.
The path was already lit.
All I had to do was lace up and walk it—nerves, doubts, and all.

I remember thinking:
If I'm going to work this much, it better be for something I care about.

Not something that made me bolt from the back office just to run the stairwell—
38 flights, two steps at a time—just to shake off the frustration.
Not something that made me vacuum my entire apartment—twice—just to feel like I was accomplishing something that didn't involve arguing over markdowns.

Retail had burned me out.
Not the people—I could handle moods, silence, defensiveness.
It was the emotional load.
The resistance.

Most shoppers didn't come in open.
They came in braced for battle.

Guarded.
Defensive.
Already explaining why nothing would fit, why they hated
bathing suits, why we probably didn't have anything for
them.

I understood.
But after decades, it wears you down.

And then—fate walked in.
Wearing gym shorts.

Literally.

I was closing up shop—breaking down displays, saying
goodbye to years of sweat equity—when a trainer I knew
from the gym walked in.
Charismatic.
Sharp.
Owner of a booming personal training company with 28
trainers and a client list that practically needed its own zip
code.

He asked if I'd come run operations.
Said I had presence.
Business sense.
Passion.

Two caveats: the pay would be crap.
And I'd have to get certified.

I thought about it for maybe 90 seconds.
Said yes.

What followed?
Two of the most financially terrifying months of my life.
Rent, groceries, gas—onto credit cards like they were
stepstools to nowhere.

But I didn't back down.
I got certified.
And walked straight into the chaos.

Twenty-eight trainers.
Over 700 clients.
And me—fresh out of swimwear retail—scheduling,
smoothing, solving.

Was I intimidated?
Of course.

These trainers had abs for days and more credentials than a
cardiologist.
But they hadn't seen what I had.
They hadn't stood in a dressing room listening to a woman
whisper that she hadn't worn a bathing suit in 15 years.
They didn't know what real vulnerability sounded like.

I did.

So, I listened.
To the pauses.
The tone.
The exhaustion behind the requests.

And I kept hearing the same thing, over and over:

"My trainer doesn't listen to me."

That was the crack in the system.
Not credentials.
Not price.
Connection.

It wasn't long before people who called in didn't want the trainer I matched them with.
They wanted me.

That's when I knew.
I didn't want to run someone else's circus.
I wanted to train.
One-on-one.
Person by person.
Heart by heart.
Glute by glute.

So, after four years of operations and part-time training—I jumped.

That was over two decades ago.
And I've never looked back.

I still believed in the work—helping people feel better in their bodies through fit, fabric, and full-on honesty.
But I was ready for a shift.

No more price tags to defend.
No more mirrors to negotiate in front of.
No more trying to make someone feel okay in a suit they never wanted to wear in the first place.

Just real people.
Real effort.
Progress you couldn't return for store credit.

And what surprised me most?
They stayed.

Not for the novelty.
For the consistency.
The relationship.

They didn't want a cheerleader.
They didn't want a drill sergeant.

They wanted someone who showed up.
Who remembered.
Who gave a damn.
Every single time.

That's the work I signed up for.
And that's the work that's kept me showing up—year after year.

I traded racks for reps.
Clearance bins for confidence.
Both jobs demanded presence.
But only one felt like truth.

And if you think that's where the hard part ended?
Let me tell you—

Leaving retail was just the warm-up.

The real work—the gritty, glorious mess of helping people wrestle with themselves—was just getting started.

Chapter 15: Power, Pain & Evolution

A Greek god of a trainer. Linda Hamilton's sculpted-yet-feminine physique—the kind she built for Terminator 2 without losing an ounce of woman in the process. And a diagnosis that, after a year of "expert" opinions, finally gave a name to what I'd been living with.

They didn't land all at once, but they arrived close enough together to feel like the universe had quietly decided, "Okay, it's time." Three separate moments, each with its own role, aligning to shape the person I was becoming—without fanfare, but with the quiet certainty that sometimes, life knows exactly what it's doing.

Part One: Enter Adonis

After Oberlin, I fell into a rhythm. Up before sunrise, dragging myself to the pool, swimming laps like I was still training AAU. Only this time, there was no coach pacing the deck, barking, "Kick harder!" or "Cut that wall time!" Just me, the water, and the echo of my own thoughts.

And let's just say, I've always been far better at giving direction than taking it. Go figure.

Lucky for me, my apartment complex came with not just a sprawling outdoor pool, but an indoor lap pool too—clean, quiet, perfect for early-morning solitude.

And right next to it? A weight room.

All glass. All mirrors. If you were into men with muscles, it was like walking into a live anatomy lesson—every delt, pec, and bicep flexing under fluorescent lights, on full display from every angle.

At the time, women were few and far between in that 1,400-square-foot jungle of treadmills, rowing machines, ellipticals, bikes, lat pulldown stations, benches, free weights, and squat racks. A few women showed up regularly, but most stuck to the cardio machines like they were tethered there by some unspoken rule. The free weights? Still prime male territory.

There were two guys I kept noticing. One older, one younger—both looking like they'd been airlifted straight from Mount Olympus. Chiseled. Imposing. The younger one? Let's call him Adonis. Because really, what else do you call a six-foot-something tower of symmetrical muscle, with a jawline sharp enough to cut tile and a smile that could melt gym-floor rubber?

The older guy—let's call him *J*—was in his fifties and looked phenomenal. Lean. Powerful. Unshakably focused, like he'd decided aging was for other people. Watching the two of them, I caught myself thinking, Damn. Is that his trainer? How does someone even get a physique like that? Is it genetics? Discipline? A deal with the devil? Or just showing up day after day until you look like that without even trying?

Nope. Trainer and client.

After watching them for a few weeks—my heart rate noticeably elevated, laps getting suspiciously slower—I had to admit the truth: my "motivation" to swim had skyrocketed. And yeah, we all know what that means.

They say curiosity killed the cat. I say curiosity got her toned and lingering at the sign-in sheet, pretending to adjust her goggles while scanning the names. Everyone had to sign in—tenants and guests—so all I needed was a time window and a reason to loiter. It wasn't hard to figure out who was who.

Turned out, the older guy—*J*—lived in the building. Adonis didn't. Adonis was the trainer.

And suddenly, I had endless reasons to "bump into" them: poolside, gym entrance, front desk. The pool and gym were connected after all, and I made certain my swims ended right when they were mid-workout. Subtle? Maybe not. Effective? Absolutely.

J was, in a word, a player. Define it however you like. I was single, curious, and very much alive. One day, it turned into a date. Then another. Before I knew it, we were "dating"—if that's what you'd call champagne-heavy dinners at the best restaurants, where he'd order the most lavish, off-menu dishes just because he could. He drove a Rolls Royce and loved to impress. He loved that at first, I seemed impressed—but not in the way he wanted.

Because here's the thing: spending piles of money on meals and cars has never been the way to my heart. I liked his company, cared about him, but attraction? Not so much.

We settled into something resembling friendship—if your friend also liked to brag that you were the only woman he ever dated who didn't sleep with him. His words, not mine.

Still, I learned plenty while watching J train. And more importantly, I knew what I wanted: Adonis to train me.

I was working my ass off at the swimwear store, juggling college loans while trying to save for retirement, and I wasn't the type to throw money around on "whims". And yet? The desire, the borderline obsession to lift with weights became a turning point, not a whim.

So, I made it happen. I hired Adonis to train me twice a week. It felt like a luxury and a necessity, all wrapped in one sweaty, perfectly symmetrical package. He fit right into my Linda Hamilton moment—and into the diagnosis that pushed me toward weightlifting for life. Plus, I was in my mid-twenties, cocky enough to think "bring it on, dude" was a real training plan.

And he did. He brought it.

Adonis trained with one philosophy: total annihilation. No mercy, no coddling, no "maybe that's enough for today." Just exercise by exercise, rep by rep, until my muscles were shaking and my mind was blissfully blank. I loved every second of it.

Walking became optional. Stairs were a personal Everest. Sitting down? An exercise in public humiliation. The next day, I didn't need to check my workout log—I could feel exactly what we'd worked on. So could anyone watching me lower myself into a chair.

And then—because there's always a then—my back blew out.

Seated rows. Too much weight. Poor form. No correction. Just brute force, ego, and a trainer too caught up in the moment to rein me in. Lower disc, partially herniated. One excruciating, life-changing lesson, served hot.

That was the end of our professional training.

But the training wasn't the only thing that ended.

From the beginning, we were into each other. Fully, undeniably, physically into each other. We'd train like animals—endorphins firing, pulses high, bodies buzzing—and then we'd take that energy and let it explode in every possible way. Yeah, it was that good.

For months, we blurred the lines between sets and sheets, sweat from the gym blending into the sweat of what came after. It was raw, charged, and completely consuming. Adonis felt a little guilty, I think—his close friendship with *J* meant he knew *J* wanted me, badly, and that it was never going to happen.

Eventually, Adonis and I parted ways—both as trainer and as lovers. We moved on, stayed on friendly terms, and lived our lives.

And for the record? I've never crossed that line with a client of my own, and I never will. It's unprofessional, unethical, and a recipe for disaster. But back then, in my twenties? It was what it was. No regrets.

And if you're wondering if I'd do it again?

I wouldn't trade what I learned from Adonis for anything.

But that wasn't the end of the story.

Because by then, I was hooked.

So, I did what I've always done when something matters: I taught myself. Everything.

Every movement. Every muscle group. Every tweak, variation, and theory I could get my hands on. I got certified, of course—because you have to in this business. But the piece of paper on the wall? That was just the baseline.

The real education started when I hit the floor.

Because not everyone moves the same. Not everyone's built the same. And not everyone wants the same outcome.

There's no such thing as "perfect form." Hell, there's no such thing as perfect—period.

Trainers are taught textbook mechanics. That's the starting point.

But I learned to adapt to the body in front of me—not the one in a manual. My clients became my curriculum.

And here's the irony: I still use the word "perfect." I say it when someone nails their form, or their focus, or just gets it right, for them.

"Perfect," to me, means it's right for you.

Is it National Academy of Whatever–approved? Probably not.

But it's working. And that's what matters.

One of my favorite clients—let's call him *A*—gave me a response to that word I'll never forget.

This was early in our training, years ago. I had just praised a set: "Perfect."

He barely blinked before shooting back:

"Char, did you expect anything less?"

I paused. Smiled. And yeah—I still say "perfect" to this day.

Every time I do, I think of that moment. That little flash of client cockiness that really meant I trust you. I've got this.

In that moment, he wasn't just a trainee.

He was a good client.

Part Two: The Linda Hamilton Revelation
Terminator 2.

Linda Hamilton. That first scene.

It's the only time in my life I've ever stayed in a theater to watch the same movie twice. That's how completely enthralled I was.

Not with the plot. Not with the effects.

With her.

Linda Hamilton.

That first scene in Terminator 2.

She's in a psych ward. White T-back tank. Fitted sweatpants. Knocking out chin-ups like she's training for a prison break—or the end of the world. Her arms. Her back. Her entire presence was cut from effort. No glamour muscles. Just earned, lived-in strength. Functional. Intentional.

And back then? Women didn't show muscle. Not in public. Not on big screens. The default female body was soft, hidden, ornamental.

Linda shattered that. She didn't just flex—she kicked open the cultural door. She gave women permission to look powerful. To be powerful. Muscular and still undeniably feminine. Sharp. Alive.

At least in my mind.

Which, let's be honest, is the one that counts, remember, my memoir.

That was it.

It was the moment.

The image didn't just change how I trained—it changed how I showed up.

Even now, I still have to remind myself: shoulders back, head high, chest open.

The shy kid? Still there sometimes, lingering in my posture.

And for the record, I'm still the person who needs a deep breath before walking into a crowded room or speaking in front of a big group. I can do it—if I muster up the courage and pull my physical and emotional act together. But don't let the muscles fool you. Confidence isn't always automatic. Sometimes, you've got to drag it out by the collar and tell it to show up.

But I walk in anyway.

Because now I know I'm seen.

And I'm proud to be.

But here's the thing about strength—sometimes it starts showing up long before you even realize you need it.

Part Three: Diagnosis and Destiny

Let's rewind—before Linda. Before Adonis. Before any of it.

I'd been dealing with pain.

Weird, chronic, always-on-the-move kind of pain. The kind that makes you feel like a walking game of symptom roulette.

One day it was my elbow. Then my knee. My neck. It jumped around like it had ADD and a mean streak.

Cue the doctor parade. Nine specialists. Nine wildly different theories.

Diet changes. Meds. Physical therapy. More meds.

There were days I could barely walk—my knees throbbed so badly it felt like bone grinding on bone. Then it would vanish... and I'd wake up unable to lift an arm. Shoulder pain so sharp it felt like someone was stabbing my rotator cuff with a serrated knife.

I'd scream into the silence:
"This is insane! What the hell is wrong with me?"

And no—it is not psychosomatic.
(But thanks for that, Dr. Brad. You really outdid yourself.)

Finally—doctor number ten.

Dr. Howard Levine. Rheumatologist. Kind face. Worn-out shoes. The kind of guy who looked like he'd been listening to people's pain for a very long time—and still cared.

He did a full exam, asked real questions, listened like he meant it. And then he gave me that look—part clinical confidence, part quiet empathy.

The "I've-seen-this-a-thousand-times" look.

"I'm almost certain it's fibromyalgia," he said. "We'll run bloodwork to confirm. But I'm telling you now: the prescription is 25 milligrams of Zoloft—and exercise, training with weight, specifically."

Zoloft.
(Sertraline hydrochloride, for the fancy folks. First FDA-approved in 1991, in case you're building a trivia team.)

I filled the prescription, started taking it, and... kept taking it. For decades.

Why? It worked.

It didn't turn me into a floating cloud of joy, but it made the fog and the edge manageable enough to function—and function well. It took me an embarrassingly long time to realize it was technically an antidepressant, but at that point? Who cared. It was part of the healing, part of the management, part of the deal.

And let's be honest: if a little Zoloft is what it takes to keep me training, working, and not screaming into the void, I'll take the damn Zoloft.

Now for the good part.

Weight training. Forever. Three times a week. Plus abs.

No discussion. No debate. No wait-and-see.

And yeah—it was bizarre. I was in my twenties, being handed a diagnosis I'd always associated with older women in orthopedic shoes and wool cardigans. It felt like I'd been dropped into the wrong demographic by accident.

But strangely? It gave me direction.

Finally—a name for the mystery.
Finally—something I could do about it.

It Was Meant to Be

So, there it was.

Adonis and *J.*
Linda Hamilton in T2.
Dr. Levine and his lifetime prescription.

The universe laid it out like a perfect triangle—and at the center?

Me.

A girl who had no idea that lifting weights would become both the literal and metaphorical foundation for the rest of her life.

The kid who thought she'd be fitting swimsuits forever, now deadlifting her way into a new future.

The shy girl, finding her voice rep by rep.
The young woman, building strength she didn't even know she'd need.

It was all there, waiting. And it was mine to claim.

Because sometimes, you don't choose the iron.
The iron chooses you.

Bonus Notes

The fibromyalgia pain? Mostly gone.

As long as I lift consistently, I feel good. Solid. Functional.

But the neck? That's another story.

The pain at the base of my neck is more than a nag—it's the engine for the cervical migraines I get almost every day. The kind no medication can fully touch. Some over-the-counter options calm it down for a bit, but nothing really fixes it. There's a chapter devoted to this story later.

It sucks.

Yet somehow, that relentless ache is still a reminder.

It's the whisper that says, "Don't stop. This is working."

And the experience? It gave me empathy. Perspective.

When clients tell me they hurt, I don't nod politely and move on.
I get it.

Pain isn't just physical. It's mental. Emotional.
It creeps into your work, your sleep, your identity.

And because I've lived it, no one gets to say I wouldn't understand.
They'd be wrong.

And I've got the receipts.

Because before I ever trained a single client, I was already in the business of bodies.
Not sculpting them—selling to them.

And most of what I'd later confront as a trainer—posture issues, insecurity, false confidence, fantasy goals—I'd already met face-to-face.
In the swimwear fitting room.

Manufacturers didn't send us promotional posters. So, we made our own.
Translation: Sunny grabbed the camera, and I squeezed into the suits.

No glam squad. No lighting crew.

Just a roll of film, a little nerve, and me doing my best not to look like I needed a cover-up—or an exit strategy.

The results?
Plastered all over the store. Life-size. Bold.

And, to our surprise? Effective.

Here's what it looked like—no filters, no apologies, no airbrushing required.

Chapter 16: Gallery — With Nerve

(*"Yes, that's me. And yes, they sold."*)

We didn't have marketing budgets. Or production crews.
We had Lycra, an old-school camera, and a whole lot of
winging it.

No stylists—unless you count Sunny. Which, to be fair, you
should. She was the stylist.
As for a director? That's where things got dicey.

She'd shout out enough posing instructions—or let's be
honest, criticisms—to make me want to scream.

Things like:
"Stop slouching."
"Stop looking straight at the camera."
"Smile, but not that much—you're not in a toothpaste ad."
"I want a three-quarter pose."
"Change your expression—it's in every single shot."
"Don't just stand there. Move."

I did my best not to fall into a shitty mood, because that
mood? It showed up in the photos like a bad headline.

A little makeup. A lot of trying not to squint.
And modesty? Yeah... she didn't get the invite.

We used an actual camera—film, remember that?
We'd shoot a roll, drop it at the photo shop, and wait a few
days for the big reveal.
No instant previews. No filters. Just hope and nerve.

Then we'd haul the decent shots—the ones where I didn't look deranged—to a print shop and blow them up. Sunny would glue them onto poster boards with her usual precision (and just enough intensity to make it an art form).

Then up they went—eye-level, bold, and impossible to miss.

They weren't art.
They were bait.

And damn... they worked.

Manufacturers rarely gave us promo material for the suits we knew would grab attention.
So, we made our own.

These weren't vanity shots. They were guerrilla marketing—swimwear-style.

Suits went up. Posters went up.
And most of the time? They came down a week later—sold out, mission accomplished.

Were they sexy? Sure.
Strategic? Hell yes.
Were they for everybody? No. And we weren't pretending otherwise.

But they made women stop. Think. Look again.
That was the goal.

We didn't shame bodies—we sold to them.
On their best day. On their not-so-best day.

We offered possibility.

And if you're flipping through this book thinking, Not for me—that's fine.
I'm not selling swimsuits anymore.
I'm selling the story.

Sunny? No way she was getting in front of the lens.

From her 50s through her 90s, she carried extra weight—
ate her stress, like most of her family did.
But she could spot a flattering cut at twenty paces, fit
anyone who walked through the door, and never let her size
slow her hustle. Not once.

"Nah," she'd say, waving me toward the backdrop.
"Let them look at you. I'll be behind the camera."

So here they are. Twenty photos from another era.

No ring lights. No filters. No retouching. No hesitation.

Just me. Suited up. On display. For the job, for the sale, for
the story.

We didn't call it branding back then.
We called it getting it done.

What you're about to see?
It's not a highlight reel.
It's a time capsule.

And yeah—that's me in every single one.

"This suit didn't whisper. It hissed—and women loved it."

"Minimal coverage. Maximum impact. Not for the faint of heart—or faint of fabric."

"Checkmate. The suit won every time."

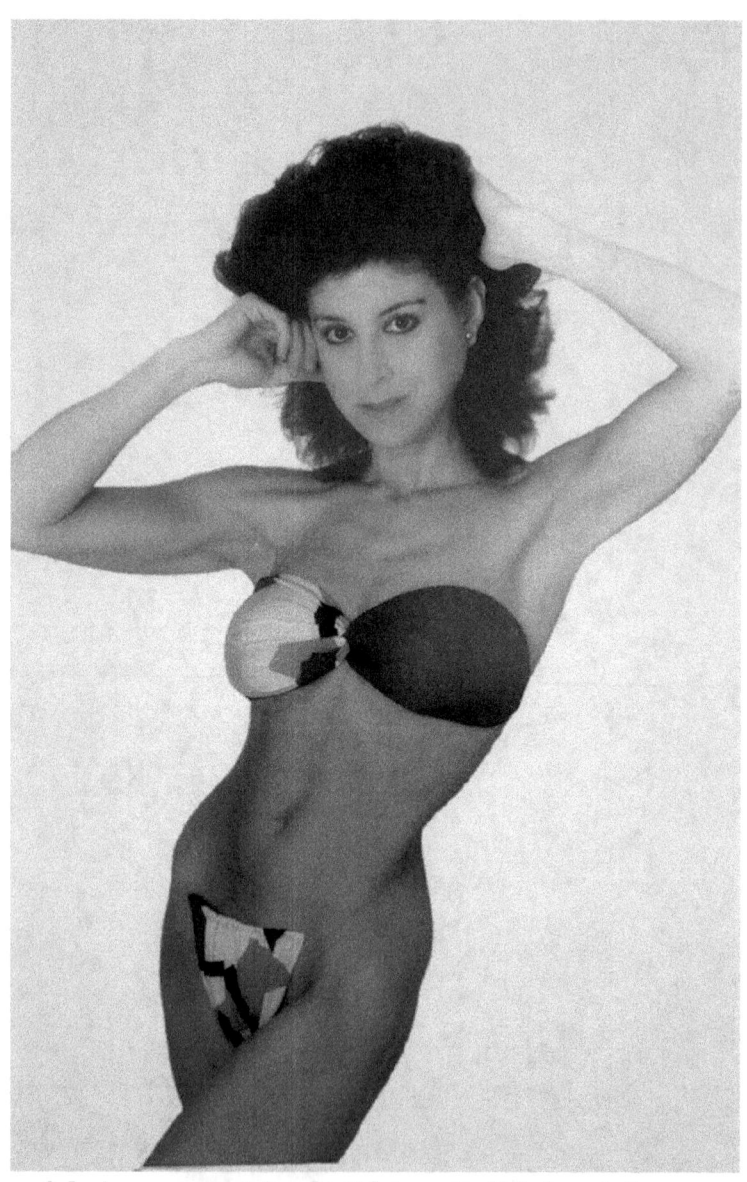

"Less fabric, more attitude. This suit didn't ask for attention—it took it."

"Minimal design. Maximum definition. And yes, that side detail sold it every time."

"Sun out, sass out. This one said: I may not be racing—but I could if I wanted to."

"Performance made personal."

"Cut to flatter. Built to own."

"Just print. Smart design. Big impact."

"Not every suit needed attitude. Some just needed a good
fit and a little structure—kind of like all of us."

"Bold print. Bigger energy. This suit sold vacations."

"Hat said hello. Suit said—watch yourself."

"Poolside, please. Preferably with champagne."

"Part mannequin, part mischief. The suit shimmered, the ladder was fake, and yes—we sold out of this one too."

"Elegance in front, curve on the sides. It didn't beg for attention—it knew it had it."

"The lighting? Studio-level. The wrap? Pure drama. The look? 100% mine."

"Second shoot. Fierce suit. Commitment-level bow. Jungle meets downtown—and owned it."

*"Worn hard. Hugged tight. Those plastic sides? Trouble—
before I was."*

"It didn't whisper. It purred."

"Swim team starter pack. All business, all gear, all me."

We didn't set out to make statements. We set out to move inventory. The posters weren't meant to provoke. They were meant to catch the eye, stall a shopper mid-step, and maybe nudge her into a dressing room she'd been avoiding. If she saw something in those photos—confidence, curves, a certain boldness—and thought, Maybe that could be me, then we'd done our job. I wasn't selling sex. I was selling fit. Fabric. Function. Something a woman could wear and feel like she owned the space she walked into. That's the image I wanted her to try on first. Understandably, not for everyone.

Sunny and I didn't sit around analyzing angles or lighting or whether a photo might one day be "too much." We picked the shot that showed the suit best. We glued it to the board. We hung it. And if the suit sold out that week? Down it came. On to the next one.

There was no hidden agenda. No filters. No soft lighting to hide behind. Just a business. A woman in a swimsuit. And a mother who knew exactly how to make it happen.

That's it. That's the story.

I sold swimsuits. I sold confidence. I sold aspiration to women in a size 10 with Lycra panels.

But what I really learned in that world?
How to see people—before they could see themselves.

Now?
I train them.
But not the way you think.

PART II: PHILOSOPHIES — TRAINING, TRUTH & TOUGH LOVE

You've seen the spandex.
Now meet the muscle and the spine.

This next stretch isn't about fabric, fittings, or what flatters under retail store lighting.
It's about what holds everything up—the invisible scaffolding behind the scenes.

These chapters lay down the philosophies, the boundaries, the well-earned opinions, and the unvarnished truths that kept me from snapping—literally or figuratively.

This is where I show you the strength behind the smile.
The mindset that's powered every session, every comeback, every early morning alarm.

Swimsuits sold.
And that mattered.
Those suits left in shopping bags, wrapped in tissue, taken home with hope.
Some became favorites, worn for summers and milestones.
Some stayed tucked away until the day felt right.

We weren't just selling spandex.
We were helping people see themselves, believe in themselves, and giving them permission to show up.

And then there was personalized training.

Training holds a different kind of weight.
Reps. Routines. Consistency. Lifestyle.
It's not a one-and-done purchase—it's a commitment. A
showing up, over and over again.

When people stayed consistent, it showed how deeply they
were willing to invest in themselves.

The store taught me how to see people.
How they stood. How they hid.
What they wanted but couldn't always say out loud.

With training, I wanted to take that further.

In the fitting room, I could help someone see themselves
for a moment.
In the workout room, I could help them become someone—
stronger, healthier, more confident. Proud of the work they
were doing.

I was tired of a system that pushed constant sales,
discounts, and next season's merchandise.
I wanted to offer something real.
Lasting.
Mine to give—no markdowns, no negotiations, no
navigating the minefield of retail, when it was always about
the person.

I became the product.
The guide.
The method.
They could take it or leave it.

But for those who stayed?
We got to work.

This next part isn't about fabric or fittings.
It's about behavior. Patterns. People.
What they carry in, what they cling to, what they fight like hell to hide.

This is what happens when you strip away the slogans, mute the playlists, and get down to the real work.

Welcome to my side of the weight room.

Every profession has its myths.
In the fitness world, they show up in motivational memes, overpriced leggings, and promises of quick fixes.

People think training is about outsourced motivation.
About discipline.
About shouting "You got this!" over a thumping playlist and calling it coaching.

They think it's about six-pack shortcuts, bikini challenges, and twenty-one-day transformations.

It's not.

It's about truth.
And truth doesn't always sell well next to a smoothie bar.

This section lays it out—what I've learned, what I've unlearned, and what I've had to say in more consults than I can count.

And let's be clear: this isn't a "how to train" book or a list of exercises to copy and paste into your workout.
Spoiler: not everyone's ready to hear it.
But if you are?
Good. Let's go.

Yes, I sold swimsuits.
But not the fantasy. Not the false promise of a perfect body in a perfect life.

What I offered were tools. A voice. A better mirror.

For some, it was a size 14 with Lycra panels and a little forgiveness in the hip.
Often, it came with a deep breath and a down-to-earth opinion—more like a statement:
You're okay. And who the hell is anyone to say otherwise?

What I really learned in that world—between the dressing rooms and the quiet apprehension—was how to see people.
Not size them up like their worth could be calculated in stretch fabric.
Not dress them for the approval of strangers.
But actually, see them. Behind the armor. Before the judgment.
In that breath-held moment where they weren't sure they were enough.

And now?
I train them.

Chapter 17: Finding My Fit

When I first thought about hiring a trainer—back before I ever became one—I wasn't looking for a cheerleader.
I didn't want someone clapping through my squats like we were at a high school pep rally. I wasn't after motivational posters in motion.
I wanted consequences.
I wanted results I could see in the mirror, feel in my posture, and carry into every room I walked into.

I was in my mid-twenties, working my retail butt off, clocking long hours on my feet, managing stress the way most people do—badly.
And still, I wanted that body. Real strength, real definition, real presence.
I thought the best way to get there was to find someone who would push me—hard, fast, no compromise.

I tried a couple trainers. One was all about education— breaking down every movement, talking muscle engagement, giving homework.
Nope. Not for me.
All that talking? I'd be asleep before the warmup.

Then came Adonis. You read his story in a prior chapter. (Not his real name, but close enough.)
He didn't coddle. He crushed. Every session was a blitz of force, sweat, and borderline punishment.
With my endorphins in warp drive, I ate it up.

Yes, I got stronger.
But I also got injured.

More than once.

Looking back, that wasn't just on him—it was on me.
I had the drive, the ambition, the reckless "let's go"
mentality.
But no governor. No brakes. No exit ramp.

And Adonis? He was happy to keep the pedal slammed
while I rode shotgun without a seatbelt.

Eventually, we parted ways.
I took the wheel myself.
Caution? Please.
I drove that body like a stolen car—twice a day, full throttle,
no seatbelt.

In the gym from 5 to 7 a.m., then back again for another
two hours in the afternoon.
Overtrained. Under-recovered. But absolutely convinced I
was doing what it took.

It wasn't until my body pushed back—hard—that I finally
started listening.

"Char," I told myself, "if you want this to be your lifestyle,
you can't destroy yourself."
That was the moment it all began to shift—from a results
junkie chasing definition to someone thinking long game.
I didn't want a transformation.
I wanted permanence.
And that meant changing how I trained, how I recovered,
and—most of all—how I thought about what strength really
looked like.

I wasn't always on my own.

For four years, I worked as the Operations Director for a company that provided in-home personal training.

The owner? A top-tier trainer with a client list full of pro basketball players.

He needed more time for the high-flyers, so he handed me everything else: scheduling, logistics, trainer wrangling, client complaints, and whatever mess landed in the cracks. That was me.

And those four years taught me more than any certification ever could.

I saw every type of training personality in action.

Some were brilliant—creative, intuitive, empathetic.

And some were a walking liability.

Push too hard. Whisper bullshit affirmations. Disappear mid-program.

Injure someone, gaslight them about it, then blame their form.

That's the circuit.

That's when I realized I had to find my own lane—not just in how I trained, but in who I chose to train.

I didn't want to train in gyms. Period.

Nothing about the sweaty locker room grunts, the bro-science debates, or the mirror-flexors screaming through "leg day" ever appealed to me.

I wasn't there to spot egos.

I was there to train bodies.

And let's be honest—I'm small.

I wasn't about to train NFL linebackers. That was never the plan.
(Though yes—there was one exception. See: The Lineman and the Stealth Cat.)

But I could train the people no one else knew what to do with.
People in recovery.
People in limbo.
People post-surgery, post-chemo, post-hope.
People whose lives didn't fit neatly into a "12-week transformation" package.

Those were my people.
Still are.

Like the neurosurgeon's wife.
That was one of the turning points.
It hit me: I wasn't just offering workouts—I was building trust with people who needed to be seen, not sold to.

My background in swimwear—those thousands of bodies, thousands of insecurities—had been the perfect education.
I'd learned to read people the way some read X-rays.
The way someone stood. The way they fidgeted. The way they avoided the mirror.
It all told me something.

That was my niche.
I just hadn't known it yet.

Here's something no one puts in the ads:

Almost everyone who lifts weights or does cardio—without well-earned breaks and small time-outs—will get a reality check from their body sooner or later.
It's not about strength.
It's about repetition.

Muscles bounce back.
Tendons? Ligaments? Joints?
They revolt. Quietly at first—then with sirens.
Connective tissue wears down. It tears. It calcifies.

Welcome to the club.
It's called arthritis.
And if you live long enough, you're invited.

That's where I come in.
My job is to build muscle around those fragile structures.
To protect the joint.
To stabilize the body.
To make sure you can get out of a car without sounding like popcorn.

I train for movement longevity.
Not six-pack abs.
Not "bikini season."
Not the fantasy bullshit that keeps the fitness industry spinning like a hamster wheel dipped in pre-workout.

Meanwhile, the rest of the world is getting blasted with advice that borders on satire:
"Drink this."
"Eat that."
"Try this equipment—it shakes the fat off!"

"Buy this supplement—it burns calories while you sleep!"
"Don't eat after 7 p.m."
"Lift like a Navy SEAL!"
"Run like a cheetah!"
"Recover like a monk!"

What the hell are people supposed to do—decode this garbage fire of advice with a Ouija board and a blender full of overpriced greens?

The fitness industry thrives on confusion.
Keep people desperate, and they'll buy whatever you're selling.
As long as it sparkles.

I'm not selling sparkle.
(Okay—maybe in accessories. I do love sparkle everywhere on everything.)
But in training?

I'm not peddling magic. I'm not dishing out illusion.
What I am offering is hope.
Not the kind you find in a bottle, a bar, or a burner workout.
The kind that's earned—with effort, repetition, a few setbacks, and a solid plan.
Real hope.
The kind that sticks.

And sometimes, people come to me saying they want six-pack abs or a bikini body.
It happens.
And I love it.

Because when they stick with it, when they put in the work, when the consistency finally pays off?
Let's just say shirts get lifted for a quick visual check—and yep, I get to see the results.
No complaints here.

And a handful of women over the years?
I've taken them out for their bikini shopping sprees as promised—part celebration, part motivation, and part comedic adventure in fitting rooms.
We'd find the suits, snap the pics, and you bet your ass there was sparkle involved.

I'm selling work.
Honest, custom-fit, often breathless, human-as-hell work.

The kind where at times, we laugh between sets
and you still curse me on the stairs the next day.

I don't promise billboard bodies.
But hell—if that's how your body turns out?
Let's get it up there.
I'll help you climb the ladder with a protein shake in one hand
and a dumbbell in the other.

I didn't stumble into this work.
I steered into it.
Deliberately. Intentionally.
With a lifetime of instincts honed from storefronts, swimwear, and hard-earned grit.

I didn't just learn direction—I chose it.
And over time, it became a straight-up calling.

The people I train?
They don't need yelling.
They don't need fixing.
They need smart programming.
Straight talk.
And yeah—sometimes a well-timed pep talk that actually
means something.

In the next few stories, you'll meet the people I've trained.
Not because they shaped me,
but because they gave me a place to apply what I know best.
How to see people.
How to show up.
And how to make strength stick.

Because this work?
It's not just about what you lift.
It's about what you carry.

Chapter 18: Adjusting the Lens

It's not about perfect reps, flawless posture, or even how I see you.
It's about how you see you.

Because most people walk in already stuck—
fixated on the part they hate,
the feature they've been taught to hide,
the thing they think disqualifies them.

In swimwear, it was always the midsection, the thighs, the arms.
In training, it's "these skinny legs," "this weak core," or "I just want to get rid of this."

I've had women with beautiful figures walk in, heads down, laser-focused on their midsection, convinced it wasn't flat enough.
I've seen men pound their fists—thud—into their thighs, spitting, "Look at these. Pathetic."

Not one of them was broken.
But nearly all of them had a story running in the background
telling them they weren't good enough.

That's the work.
Not just strengthening the body—
adjusting the lens.

One thing people figure out pretty quickly about me:
when I ask, "How are you?" I actually mean it.

It's not small talk.
It's not a throwaway greeting like a breath mint.
I ask because I care.

Whether it's someone I've trained for fifteen years
or someone I bump into under the harsh glow of grocery
store lights,
people seem to know I'm not wasting my breath.

And because they know I care, they share.

Physical pain.
Emotional grief.
A fight with their kid.
A diagnosis they're still trying to process.

I hear it all.
And here's the kicker—I remember it.

Not just the big stuff either.
The surgery dates.
The pet names that echo in my head.
The weird foot pain that only shows up when it rains.

Some clients joke that I should really get a life of my own,
since I somehow manage to remember more about their
lives than they do.

I laugh—but they're not wrong.
My head's a crowded closet,
full of other people's timelines, habits, and orthopedic
quirks.

And I wouldn't have it any other way.
Because that's how trust is built.
Not just through reps and stretches—
but through presence.

Through showing up as a human being,
not some chipper, calorie-counting drill sergeant in
workout pants.

And no, I'm not on some high horse.
I've got my own crap.

I'll share it when it matters—
when it makes someone feel less alone, less judged.

I've spent most of my life being judged,
especially in this industry.

So yeah—I know how heavy it feels.
I've had to push through that judgment.
And in the process, I learned how to walk the line between
vulnerability and strength.

That's what I bring into the room.
Every session.
Every time.

It's the same thing I brought when I was fitting women in
bathing suits—
hundreds, probably thousands, over the years.

And trust me:

people will tell you more about themselves in a fitting room
than they ever will in therapy.

Especially under the buzz of fluorescent lights
and the cold honesty of a three-way mirror.

They'd walk in practically defeated.

If someone told me they hated their thighs or their jiggly
triceps—
or said they weren't beautiful, or handsome,
or that their gut was too big or their shoulders too narrow—
I didn't argue.

I didn't gaslight them into feeling better.
I didn't toss out a chirpy, "Nooo, you're gorgeous!" just to
kiss ass.
People know when you're faking it.

What I'd say was:
"I see where you're coming from."
"Yeah, I get why that would make you uncomfortable."
"Let's see how we can lessen the visuals and shift the focus."

And then I'd do just that.

I'd find a suit that brought out their skin tone,
highlighted the bustline,
flattered the waist,
lifted the mood.

We'd focus on what was right—
not what they wanted to erase.

Then came the rack of cover-ups—sarongs, wraps, tunics, you name it—
sliding across the metal bar with a soft rattle, waiting to be chosen.

Something to toss on before and after the swim.
Something that made them feel like they owned the beach instead of hiding from it.

And guess what?
That small shift?

It changed people.

Because it wasn't just about swimsuits.
It was about permission.

Permission to be seen.
To feel good.
To stop apologizing for the parts of yourself that haven't been airbrushed.

I'd like to think every personal interaction I had in that fitting room
added something of value to someone's life.

Something they could take with them—
maybe quietly, maybe much later—
and reassess.

To think twice before falling back into the trap society sets for us all:

the self-insecurity machine that runs on comparison,
shame, and airbrushed lies.

If I gave someone even a moment to pause that spiral and
see themselves differently—
then it was worth it.

That's what I do as a trainer, too.

I don't promise miracles.
I'm not in the magic business.

What I offer is reality—with empathy.
I see what people won't say.
And I meet them exactly where they are—
no judgment, no agenda.

From there, we move forward.
One step.
One rep.
One conversation at a time.

It's a turning point.
And not just emotionally.

So, if your lens is a little smudged—
by insecurity,
by old stories,
by what you think disqualifies you?

Maybe it's time to give it a wipe.
That's where real change starts.

Of course, seeing yourself clearly—
and helping you get there—
comes with a price.

Because showing up like this, every session, every time?

It's not cheap.

Chapter 19: You Charge What?

What you're signing up for
isn't some glorified gym babysitter
who counts to ten and pats you on the back
for not dying under a barbell.

You're getting me—
decades deep in this work.

So, when you ask:
"You charge what?"
Here's what I say:

You're paying for almost 30 years of lived expertise.
For judgment shaped by time, testing, and ongoing
learning—
not a weekend workshop.

You're paying for injury prevention.
For muscle understanding.
For mind-body strategy.
For accountability.
For honesty.

Because you're not just paying for my time.
You're investing in your life.
You're paying for the trainer who will see you.
Who will remember your story.
Who won't let you vanish into another gimmick
or a glossy program with zero substance.

I'm not just trained.

I'm forged.

Forged through experience,
through watching what works and what breaks people
down,
through a relentless focus on what happens
when the right tools finally meet the right mindset.

I've helped people lose a hundred pounds—
without losing themselves in the process.

I've trained clients well into their nineties—
clients who now walk into a room like they own it,
not shrink from it.

I've worked with post-op men
rebuilding real-world strength—
not just to check a box for a physical therapist,
but to actually live again.

I've seen thin arms grow capable,
cautious shoulders grow powerful,
and strong-willed people
finally match their physical strength
to the force of their personality.

That's the kind of transformation I help create.

It's not about hype.
It's about what holds—years later.

This isn't a gig for me.
It's a life.

And it's priced accordingly.

Before anyone acts scandalized,
let's look at where people toss money without blinking:

- $17 green juices that taste like blended grass and regret
- $200 workout gear (spoiler: I don't own any)
- Subscription boxes full of protein dust and delusion
- Tasting-menu dinners that rack up hundreds per person—
washed down with cocktails and dessert, but somehow
that's "worth it"

But invest in someone
who might help them stand up without pain in ten years?

Suddenly, it's like I've asked them to sell a kidney.

I've seen it all—
Women gasping like I just insulted their firstborn.
Men reaching for their second martini,
needing something strong to process the number.

Here's what I tell them:

Many of my clients drop thousands—plural—on vacations
every year.
World cruises. Safaris. Wine tours in Tuscany.

And hey—live your life.
I'm not here to knock that.

But training with me twice a week, consistently, over the
course of months?

Costs less than one of those getaways.

And here's the kicker:
The body you're building with me?
That's what helps you actually enjoy those vacations—
walk the cobblestones, hike the ruins,
lift your carry-on and make it to dessert without a heating
pad.

Because what good is first class to France
if your back gives out before baggage claim?

I'm self-employed.
Which means I pay self-employment tax,
cover my own business expenses, certifications, insurance—
everything the IRS doesn't care about.

There's no gym cutting me a check.
No corporate logo footing the bill for my health care.

Just me—showing up, year after year,
client after client—
with care, with humor,
and zero tolerance for BS.

I don't train clients once or twice,
hand them a resistance band,
and wave goodbye with a "You got this!"

It doesn't work that way.

It takes time—
Time to understand how your body responds to movement.

Time to modify around injuries or surgical healing.
Time to adjust reps, weight, and tempo on the fly.
Time to build trust.
Time to see real change.

And no—I don't use a stopwatch.
This isn't a race.
And no, I don't build cardio into your session.
That's your homework.

And that's why I charge what I charge:
because when you walk out of my space,
you'll stand taller, move stronger,
and carry yourself like someone who finally knows their
own worth.

Not Part of the Deal

• A stopwatch
• A glorified cardio class
• A half-hearted pep talk from someone already planning
their next TikTok reel

This is one-on-one, all-in, no-BS care.
So yeah—
I charge what I charge.

And if that makes you blink?
Blink twice.
Then get in line.

How This Works

When someone sits down for a consultation, I give it to them straight.
We talk goals, health history, and realities.
What they want—
and what I can actually deliver.

I know my training works—if people do their part.
No magic timelines.
No one-size-fits-all plans.
No co-dependence unless that's what they need—
and can afford.

If they can't or don't want a trainer forever?
I get it.
We'll make a plan that works.

I talk big and walk bigger because I care.
And at times, you'll find me entertaining.

I'll get you where you want to go—
within reason,
with your participation.

But there are two dealbreakers.
And I usually look my male clients straight in the eye when I say this:

First: I talk.
Not gossip. Not fluff.
But relevant, real-life talk.
I connect.
It's part of how I train.

Second: My counting isn't always precise.
I get lost between one and three—
because while I'm watching your form,
planning the next move,
listening to what you said,
and challenging what you didn't,
the numbers sometimes slip.

But it evens out by the end.
Trust me.

If either of those is going to be a problem?
We're not going to be a good fit.

And for the ones who are a fit?
They show up.
Not always eagerly.
But they show up anyway.

More Than Reps

• A program built specifically for you—your body, your
goals, your life
• Adjustments made in real time, based on how you walk in
the door
• A human, compared to a computer-generated workout,
who actually remembers what you're going through—
physically, emotionally, hormonally
• A trainer who refuses to injure you just to prove
something or impress anyone
• And with any luck, someone who won't bore you to death
in the process

Training Attire: TBD

I don't show up in $200 leggings with a matching
cucumber water bottle.
Half the time, when someone compliments something I'm
wearing,
I grin and say, "Thanks—Walmart."

I dress for function and comfort, and—this part matters—
for the person I'm working with.

New female client? Extremely overweight?
I'm not walking in wearing something tight and showy.
This isn't about me—it's about her comfort, her focus, and
her sense of safety.

Male client with a wandering eye?
I'm not showing up in a low-cut tank.
You came here for results, not a distraction.

I'm here to deliver your workout—
not become the show.

But longtime clients—those who've made me part of their
lifestyle?
I'll wear what I want.
Quirky. Bold. Fun.

Because by then, we've earned that space together.
There's trust.
There's history.
There's freedom to just be—without explanation.

After all that, what I wear barely makes it through the front door. It doesn't matter how coordinated my outfit is—once I cross that threshold, I get taken out by the real stars of the session: dogs who think I'm theirs, cats who think I'm late, and the occasional parrot who swears at me before the client even gets a word in.

Chapter 20: Noses, Paws & Kisses

They showed up.
They got through it.
They felt better.

Let's just get this out of the way:
Many of my clients don't look forward to the workouts with
bated breath. They know what's in store. (However, there
are always one or two.)

Never did. Still don't.
Not even after twenty years or a thousand sessions.

I've spent most of my training career either walking into
their homes or having them show up at mine.
And yet—every time—they showed up.
Or left the door unlocked so I could walk in, unannounced,
like some domestic intruder bearing resistance bands.

And the first greeting?
Almost never from the client.

It was the dog—tail wagging, foot tapping, joy on paws.
Or the cat, who emerged from wherever cats vanish to when
they're off-duty.
In cat terms, just showing up for a glance and a leg bump is
practically a standing ovation.

"Hi, Char, I see you," said the blinking, slow-motion head
turn from the hallway shelf.
That's affection—feline-style.

There was the bulldog who barreled toward me like I was a pork chop in leggings.

The aloof Siamese who perched at the edge of the exercise mat, one paw extended like royalty deciding whether or not to bless me.

The mutt mix who couldn't care less about fetch but lived for our post-session cooldown.

And the dogs who thought "squat" meant jump up and lick her face! every single time.

(They weren't wrong.)

The human, on the other hand?

"Hey. Come in."

That was if they didn't just holler from the couch while I let myself in and got the full welcome from their four-legged emissary.

No one ever shouted, "Char! So good to see you! Come on in! What a treat!"

Nope.

That wasn't the vibe.

And I didn't need it to be.

I never took on clients who wanted their hands held or their egos stroked.

I didn't work with people who hired a trainer to accessorize their self-image—like a Peloton with a pulse.

I trained the ones who needed what I brought:

The structure.

The relentless showing up.

The ability to be an unflinching mirror—while still giving a damn.

They didn't want to train.
But they did it anyway.

Every so often, one of them would say out loud what most were thinking:

"I can't believe I'm paying her to make me do something I hate."
"I'm a successful person... why do I still need her to get this done?"
"She's here again? God help me."

And I never—not once—took it personally.
I got it.

You're tired.
You're vulnerable.
You're in your own home, wearing the kind of clothing you'd never wear in public—certainly not in front of anyone but me.
The trainer.
The one telling you to do something you already hate.

Who the hell feels excited about that?

Yet after the workouts?
After the lunges, the core work, and the inevitable argument about whether I count too fast?

The smiles were real.
The thank-yous—if they came—were calm, but honest.
The hugs happened, too.

And the animals?
Always consistent.
Dog kisses. Cat tail swipes.
The occasional butt wiggle of happiness.

Sometimes I'd leave wondering if there was a "Kick Me"
sign taped to my back—judging by the pleased looks on
their faces.

But I knew what it meant:
They did it.
They showed up.
They got through their workout.
They felt better.

No big speeches.
No social media posts.
Just another small, private victory—shared between me, a
client, and their fur-covered support squad.

And here's the thing—
Even the ones who groaned, griped, and gave me the eye-
rolling face from mid-squat?

They felt good to have trained. *"I wanted to cancel. Glad I
didn't."*

Of Note:
Many of them stayed committed when they left town.

Not always.
But enough to deserve a mention.

If they were traveling for more than a couple of weeks and staying in one place longer than a few days, they usually tried to keep training.
I gave them credit for that.
Still do.

One longtime client splits her time between Bethesda and Las Vegas—a three-hour time difference.
She doesn't want to miss a session.
So, I adjust my schedule when I can, sliding her into a different slot depending on where and "when" she is.
It's not always convenient—for either of us.
But she shows up.

Another client spends six weeks in Venice, periodically.
And yes—we built a schedule that worked, even six hours ahead of DC time.
While gondolas glided past his window, we were doing "modified" dumbbell rows.

No complaints.
No drama.

I've had sessions with clients in Madrid, London, Pacific Palisades, Miami, and New York City.
These weren't vacation workouts.
No beachside burpees for Instagram.
No filtered flexing by the hotel pool.
Just people who wanted to keep showing up for themselves—even if they'd rather not.

And I met them there.
Time zone, jet lag, flaky Wi-Fi and all.

Sometimes, they brought resistance bands or sliders—
And no, not the mini burger kind.
But most of the time, especially overseas, they brought
nothing.
We used whatever was around.
Which, often, was exactly that—nothing.

I don't need dumbbells to challenge a body.
Many clients don't want to train off a hotel room floor—
even with towels stacked like a makeshift mat.
Can't blame them.

So, we got creative.
A straight-back chair.
A bed.
A windowsill.
A door frame.
A countertop.
Bodyweight.

Risk is always top of mind—especially with tight spaces,
unstable surfaces, and aging joints.
But with enough care?
You can get real work done.

And here's the bonus—
Sometimes, they'd train in front of wide windows, on
balconies, even outside.
And for those workouts, I felt like a world traveler.
Madrid rooftops.

London gardens.
Sunrise in Miami.
A canal in Venice.

I wasn't on vacation—
But I had a front-row seat to their lives.
Their world, from my screen, as they committed to doing
the thing they swore they hated—again.

That's what commitment looks like.
Not a side-by-side photo collage.
Not motivational quotes and matching gym outfits.
Not a fridge full of Tupperware meals with organic protein
and macro precision.

It's showing up—
At the wrong hour, in the wrong time zone,
with no gear, no fanfare,
to sweat it out with someone who already knows your
excuses
and doesn't buy a single one.

Because when it clicks—
when trainer and client actually sync up—
that's when it work; effective and efficient.

Chapter 21: Communication Is Key

When trainers miss the point—and how gender dynamics complicate everything.

The real secret in training?
While the workout is important,
It's the match.

Yes, form matters. Programming matters.
But if the energy's off? If the dynamic is wrong? If trust never clicks into place?
Forget it.
You're wasting your breath—and your money.

Women often came in with insecurities they weren't about to unpack with a male trainer.
She hated her ass. Or her thighs. Or the way her arms jiggled when she waved.
That wasn't a conversation she wanted to have with a guy who's never lived in a female body.
And definitely not one who'd answer, "No way! Your butt's perfect!"

Even if he meant well, she didn't want a compliment.
She wanted strategy.
Understanding.
Room to name what bothered her—without judgment.
Not a glib reassurance that skipped over the very thing she was trying to voice.

In all my years of private training, I've never had a male client say:

"Could you please focus on my inner thighs? I really want them tighter."
Not once.

And yet, I've communicated with men who refused to admit weakness in front of another man.
If the weight he was asked to lift was more than he could handle safely?
He'd grunt. Grind. Maybe even hurt himself.
But say, "I can't"?
Nope.
To some guys, especially in front of another guy,
"I can't" = "I'm not enough."

That competitive tension?
It's always just under the surface.

And yes—sometimes the reverse happens too.
There are still men who won't be trained by a woman.
See: The Disclaimer Guy.
You'll get the picture.

Sometimes it works.
Sometimes it doesn't.

I knew from years of fitting women in swimwear—and working with men too—
that gender dynamics affect comfort, communication, and whether someone lets themselves be truly seen.

I saw it again when I thought about hiring the "older male trainer" who taught like a professor and counted like a metronome.

Great guy. Solid trainer.
Just not the right fit. Not for me. Not then.

Then again—take Adonis.
Handsome. Jacked. Tough as nails.
That was motivation all on its own.
(And let's be honest—sometimes that does count.)

There's also something to be said for environment.
Some clients—male or female—simply feel more at ease
training with someone of the same gender,
in the privacy of their own home.
No crowd.
No gym performance.
Just you, them, and the work.

And others? A hard-core gym.

Half my client base is male.
They're sharp. Hard-working. Consistent.
They show up, they sweat, and they treat me—and the
work—with respect.

And that's the thing.
When it works, it really works.

There was one consistent exception for me:
Girls aged 13 to 23.

Maybe I reminded them of their mom.
Maybe I looked "too fit."
Maybe the last thing they wanted was another adult telling
them what to do in spandex.

Who knows?

All I could do was adapt.
Pull back the pressure.
Change the language.
Give them space.

Because chemistry isn't just about male or female.
Trainer or client.
It's about timing.
Maturity.
Vulnerability.
Ego.
Energy.

Men. Women.
We're different.
Not better. Not worse.
Just different.

And if you pay attention—if you really listen—you'll figure
out how to train them.
Not by barking cues.
Not by forcing your formula on every body like one-size-
fits-all spandex.

But by leading with connection.

Connection first.
Cues second.

That's how the real work begins.

Because once trust is in place, it's only a matter of time
before they point to something—
midsection, thighs, arms—
and ask the question they've been carrying for years:

"Can you get rid of this?"

Chapter 22: Can You Get Rid of This?

Some clients walk in crystal clear.
They want to bulk up, build muscle, lean out through the midsection, improve posture, or ease chronic pain.

Others speak in buzzwords they've picked up over time.
Not a performance—just the best language they've got.

And that's fair.
They're not trainers. They're not supposed to know the mechanics of body transformation.
That's my job.

So, here's how I respond:

"You tell me what your goals are. I'll tell you what I think is possible. And one more thing—in the nicest way—if your goals change, you need to tell me. Right when they change. Because if you stop doing your part and expect me to keep doing mine like nothing's shifted? That's not a partnership. That's not training. That's wasting both our time."

I say it calmly.
Directly.

Because if I'm working my ass off for someone who's quietly checked out—just coasting on the fact that I'm getting paid?
That doesn't last.

I'm not a slot machine you feed money into and hope for magic.

But it happens.
The cardio fades.
The food gets sloppy.
The focus drifts.
And suddenly, they're relying on the presence of a trainer instead of participating in their own progress.

One of my first referrals was a woman with a powerful career, a high-profile husband, two great kids—and a plan.
A real one.
She said, straight-faced:

"I want to lose 40 pounds, get as fit as I can—and then I'm getting plastic surgery for the rest."

No drama.
No denial.
No delusion.

She didn't want fantasy.
She wanted results.
And I respected the hell out of that.

She understood the order of operations:
Do the work. Then see the surgeon.

Not everyone's that clear.

For a while, I knew of the top six plastic surgeons in the region—by gossip, in many cases seeing the results of their work.
However, not in direct contact.

Clients talked about them like celebrity chefs with scalpel sets.

Some of those surgeons I respected—especially the ones who told women,
"Lose the weight first. Then we'll talk."

That? That was integrity.

Because when you skip the "do the work" part, the weight doesn't stay gone.
When the fat comes back, it doesn't knock.
It slides in like a bad houseguest—takes over new spots and makes itself comfortable.

I've seen liposuction results go sideways—fast.
Weird pockets of fat.
Cottage cheese texture.
Skin puckering.
Distortion.

Still, if a client came to me and said,
"I'm doing this for me"—and meant it?
I'd back them.
Fully. After they've done their part.

I get it.
Do what makes you feel stronger, more functional, more you.

But if you're doing it to become a shinier, smoother, more "desirable" version of yourself for a world that never saw you clearly to begin with?
Let's take a beat.

If you want to talk, I'm here.
Because you don't owe that world a damn thing.
Not your waistline.
Not your face.
Not your paycheck spent chasing someone else's version of better.

What I Can (and Cannot) Do

Let's be clear about the difference.

What I can do:
• Help you build muscle
• Increase strength and mobility
• Improve posture, flexibility, and balance
• Teach you to train safely and consistently
• Hold you accountable—with humor and without bullshit

What I can't do:
• Tighten loose skin
• Make your boobs perkier
• Give you the backside of a Kardashian
• Melt your double chin
• Erase the jiggle under your arms

That last one's a classic.
Women raise their arms, flap the underside, and say:
"See this? Can you get rid of it?"
"Sure," I say. "Lower your arm and stop flapping it around. No one'll notice a thing."

Spoiler: never lost a client over that line.
Most of them laugh—and keep training.

Here's the truth:
You can build muscle.
You can improve shape, strength, and posture.
But sagging skin?
That's biology, not laziness.

And abs?
Everybody wants a tight, flat, sculpted core.
Here's what I tell them:
"If there's fat or loose skin sitting on top, no amount of
abdominal work will make it disappear."

Abs are a combo plate:
Smart movement.
Smarter food choices.
And—sorry—a sprinkle of genetic luck.

More than anything, it's the holy trinity:
Strength training, cardio, and sustainable eating.

Not punishment.
Just patterns.

The Bottom Line

I'm not here to shame anyone out of wanting change.
Wanting to look better—or feel better—isn't vain.
It's human.

But if we're going to work together, you need to know
what's possible.
What's sustainable.
And what's real.

Thinking about surgery because your eyelids are drooping into your vision?
Your back aches from your boobs hanging down to your waist?
Go for it.

I'll "support" you—not literally.

But if you're chasing a version of you that was never yours to begin with—
Trying to "fix" yourself to fit a culture that already edits you out?

I can't deliver perfect.
I don't offer illusion.
But I can help you build something healthier.
Stronger.
More capable.
More honest.

Something that still holds up when you're not sucking in your gut or filtering yourself into invisibility.

This work?
It's slow.
Sometimes hard as hell.

It doesn't sparkle.
It doesn't trend.
But if you're doing it for you—
Not because someone else said you should—
Then it's worth every damn second.

And just when you think this is only about thighs, waistlines, or flabby arms—

You meet someone who reminds you it's also about who gets heard.
And who gets erased.
About what the world says you're allowed to say, see, or be—
And what it will quietly edit out if you refuse to play along.

That's where *L* comes in.

Chapter 23: Edited Out

The newsroom. The hallway. And what happens when your face doesn't fit the frame.

She delivered the news.
But her face didn't deliver ratings.
So, they cut her.

And I watched the whole system do what it always does—
Edit out the truth.

Let's talk about *L*.

She was a national news correspondent. Prime time.
Multiple nights a week.
The kind of woman whose voice could silence a room—and whose brain could fillet a senator mid-lie.
That sharp.

She hired me to keep her strong. Twice a week. In her home. No frills.
While most clients asked about calories or cellulite, *L* asked about deadlines, foreign correspondents, and why the world was on fire again this week.
I liked her immediately.

Blunt. Smart. Politically wired.
Zero tolerance for fluff—not in language, not in workouts, not in herself.

She also happened to be—how do we say this nicely?
Not what the camera wants.

And I mean that in the brutal, bullshit sense of media optics.

Overweight by thirty pounds, easily.
No makeup.
Short hair.
Didn't "smile more."
Didn't package herself for the screen.
Didn't apologize for it either.

She was not attractive by social media's definition.
She refused to conform.
And she paid for that.

Eventually, months into training, after building trust, I asked—quietly, off-script from lunges and squats:
"L, have you ever considered... I don't know... playing the camera game a bit? A little makeup? A little glam? It might open more assignments..."

She didn't even blink.
"I'm not here to be a Barbie doll. I'm here to report facts."

And she was.
That was her rebellion.
But rebellion has a cost.

She started getting passed over.
Shoots she should've nailed went to fresh-faced twenty-somethings in tight dresses with TikTok-ready cheekbones.
Despite her experience.
Despite her talent.
Despite her mind.

Eventually, the network nudged her into early retirement.
No fanfare.
No scandal.
Just the quiet editing-out of a woman who wouldn't bend.

But this isn't just about media bias.
It's also about the things we see coming—
The warnings we try to give—
And how often we're told we're being dramatic.

Let me back up.

It was sometime in 2001.
L and I were still training regularly.

Meanwhile, back at my apartment complex—your standard, suburban, close-to-D.C. building with too many renters and not enough owners—I started noticing something odd.

Not once or twice.
Night after night.
Approximately between 2 and 4 a.m.

Our laundry room, one per floor, was located near a particular apartment. The activity there caught my eye. These early hours—prime time for doing wash undisturbed—were all mine.

A group of young men—dark-skinned, well-dressed, clean-cut, like they'd been plucked from an Abercrombie ad minus the gorgeous grins—would show up at the apartment across from the elevator on my floor.

241

No women.
No takeout bags.
No books. No laptops.

They'd knock, get let in quietly, and disappear behind the door.

Then they'd leave—sometimes hours later, sometimes the next morning—one or two at a time, same clothes, empty arms.

It didn't add up.
Eleven guys in a 650-square-foot unit? In this neighborhood?
Why not move eight miles out and pay half the rent for twice the space?

And what were they doing?
Studying without books?
Socializing without food or alcohol?
Coordinating something without a single digital device?

I tried to logic my way out of it, but my gut wouldn't shut up.

So, I asked *L.*
She was a journalist. If anyone could help me connect the dots, it was her.

"Maybe they're foreign students," she offered. Cautious.
"Pooling resources," she added.

She was trying to make sense of the details I offered. But I could tell—she was unsettled too.

Still, what could we do?

I went to building management. Got brushed off.
"What are you doing up at that hour?"
I told them I liked doing laundry late.
No lines. No waiting.

Their response?
"Get a life, young woman."
Nice.

I wasn't trying to start a witch hunt.
I just couldn't ignore what I was seeing.

The behavior.
The frequency.
The anonymity.
The proximity to Walter Reed.
The lightning-fast Beltway access.

It all felt wrong.

Eventually, I went to the local police station.
Told them what I knew.
Names? No.
License plates? Nope.

But I had details. Dates. Patterns.
Gut instincts wrapped in a trainer's observational discipline.

They nodded, took notes, and sent me on my way.

Then one day, mid-session with *L*, she turned to me
casually, wiping sweat from her brow, and said:
"Hey Char, you haven't mentioned those guys in a while.
Any sightings?"

I paused.
"Actually, no. Now that you mention it—haven't seen them
in over a week. Maybe they moved."

I left her house.
Got in my car.
Turned on the radio.
And heard the world unravel.

Planes. Towers. Fire. The Pentagon.

I drove home in silence, cancelled my next two clients,
heart racing.
Parked. Rushed upstairs.
Climbed onto my stationary bike and flipped on the TV.

Couldn't sit.
Couldn't stand.
Just pedaled. And watched. And stared.

Then the pictures of the terrorists started to appear.

And slowly, recognition kicked me in the gut.

I recalled some of those faces.

It took hours. The beards threw me.
But the structure—the jawlines, the brows—I recognized them.
Not from the news.
From my hallway.

I called *L.* Shaking.
She patched me through to a contact—someone at the CIA.

They got on the phone immediately.
No pleasantries. Just questions:

"Who did the apartment belong to?"
"Do you have names?"
"What vehicles did they drive?"
"Did you get a plate?"

I snapped.
"Who the hell do you think I am? I'm a personal trainer, not the NSA."

For weeks, months, years, I carried this strange, simmering guilt.
Not survivor's guilt—something else.
A civic failure.

Like I saw something, said something—and still couldn't stop it.
Like I wasn't convincing enough. Loud enough.
Valuable enough.

And the irony?

L had once been the gatekeeper of the nation's news.
She knew how stories got picked—and how they got buried.
She knew exactly what happened when a woman didn't look the part.

And now, here I was.
A trainer with a gut instinct.
Dismissed in exactly the same way.

Too ordinary to take seriously.
Too female to be a credible threat.

Perhaps I am placing too much emphasis on my gender.
Others, men too, may have tried to report suspicious activity. And they too, were ignored.

L and I lost touch not long after.
She faded from the screen the same way those men had disappeared down the hallway—quietly.
No grand announcement.
No ticker-tape exit.
Just... gone.

(This is not to say their final exit was quiet. IT WAS NOT!)

Because when you don't play the visual game, the world changes the channel.
And when you do speak up—but you're not the "right" kind of voice?
Your warning gets shelved.
Right next to your credibility.

Here's the thing I keep coming back to:

L was cut for not looking the part.
And I was ignored for not being the part.

She had the brains, the journalistic firepower, the facts—
but no lip gloss.
I had the street-level observation, the timing, the gut—but
no badge, no clearance, no face the system respects.

We were both edited out of the frame in our own ways.

And the cruel joke?

In the end, we were trying to do the same thing:
Tell the truth before it's too late.

But the truth in this country wears makeup, stays thin, and
carries a clipboard.
Everyone else?
We're just background noise.

But being ignored doesn't mean you disappear.

Sometimes it means you rewrite the script—
and sing your own damn version out loud.

So no, I wasn't here for the show.
And I sure as hell wasn't here for the job interview.
I was here to work.

Chapter 24: Not Here for the Job Interview

I don't show up to a consultation dressed like I'm waiting for HR to call my name. Because this isn't an interview.

It's a test.
A two-way one.
To see if you can handle me—and if I can handle you.
If our goals, personalities, and schedules line up enough that we can do the work without killing each other.

First thing I'll tell you? Try one session before you commit to anything. You need to feel what this is—not just sign up for it like you're buying a blender.

Do I wear workout clothes? Always. Day one. Year ten. Sometimes loud and colorful, sometimes black from head to toe. If you spot a logo, it's because it fits, not because I'm selling it.

But this isn't about my outfit. It's about making one thing clear:

Some people want the fantasy.
They want a trainer who's an accessory—perfectly curated outfit, motivational slogans, and a sculpted body waiting to be photographed mid-lunge for Instagram.

That's not me.

I'm not here to be your prop.
Not here to accessorize your self-image or give you something to brag about over a $17 salad.

And I'm definitely not here to count reps with a fake smile
while you phone it in.

I'm here to make you stronger. Period.
To get your form right, keep your back from blowing out,
teach you how to pick up weight without trashing your
knees, and call you out—always with a little humor—when
you're wasting my time and yours.

I don't show up to look the part.
I show up to do my part.
Not for a photo op.
For the work.

And if you're ready to work—really work—then we start.

Who am I?
I'm caring. Perceptive. Supportive when it's earned.
And about as nonjudgmental as a human without a halo
can get.

I don't work in gyms.
I work in private spaces. Yours or mine.
No gawkers. No mirrors doubling as insecurity billboards.
Just you, me, and the work.

My humor's dry.
My patience for games? Even drier.
I'm direct, strong-minded, and allergic to passive-
aggressive anything.

If we're working together, we're moving forward.
Not someday. Not when you "feel like it."

And if that means a session stops cold so you can unload a week's worth of stress? Fine.
We'll lift through it.

Perfect? No. Not even close.

But I show up real.
And that's a better start than most people ever get.

What I've Done (That Actually Matters)

I spent years in a DC swimwear shop, and the job was never just about suits.
It was about fitting bodies—all kinds. Olympians. New moms. Post-op patients. Teenagers who wanted to vanish. Men who never thought they'd set foot in a store like that. Shy, snarky, hard-to-please.

Retail isn't glamorous. It's a ringside seat to what happens when a mirror feels like a firing squad.

Those years behind the counter taught me everything I use now:
How people armor up when they feel exposed.
How a shoulder shrug can be a white flag.
How to fix a problem without shaming someone into submission.
How to keep a room safe while someone's half-naked under fluorescent lights, trying not to disappear.

Trust doesn't come from flattery.
It comes from being honest—even when it stings.

Every body is a story, not a problem.
Help them feel seen, not scrutinized.

I walked away from the racks and took those lessons with me.
Into fitness. Into one-on-one rooms with no slogans, no hiding.
Just one plan. One person. One chance to quiet the voice in someone's head that's crueler than any mirror.

This isn't a job interview.
It's the résumé of someone who's been in the trenches of other people's battles—and knows how to make sure they walk out standing taller than when they walked in.

What I Brought With Me

When I left retail for private training, I wanted no part of the slogans, the megaphones, the beast-mode cult. I wanted something real.

Here's what happens when someone sits across from me—
or shows up on a screen:
I can see it.
Where it hurts. What's overcompensating. Where stress, imbalance, and old injuries have carved themselves into posture, breath, and hesitation.

But seeing isn't guessing.
I listen.
Before we start. While we work. As things change.

Whatever shape, scar, diagnosis, or disconnect someone brings in—I want to hear it.
I want to watch how it moves, how it breathes, how it tells the truth without a single word.

Words matter too. They tell me what's been ignored, what's been tried, what's been broken.
Because before we can build anything, we need to know where we're standing—and where we're going.

If training with me works, it's not because I shout louder.
It's because I strip away every assumption, every judgment, and meet you exactly where you are.

Experience isn't a tagline. It's repetition. Reflection.
Showing up when things are messy.

I've worked with chronic conditions, post-surgical bodies, and pain patterns most trainers never see.
Clients don't churn through.
They stay.
They evolve.
They come back stronger.

Progress doesn't always show up in the mirror.
Sometimes it's quieter knees. Better sleep.
Sometimes it's the courage to trust yourself again.

I don't just train bodies.
I train the people living inside them.
And I never forget how heavy that life can be.

Clients I've Trained

I've worked with newspaper columnists, anchors, lawyers, teachers, and surgeons. Retirees who train harder than most twenty-somethings. Moms, dads, post-surgical rebuilds. Kids whose muscles don't line up with their will.

People starting over—after injury, after childbirth, after heartbreak.

If you've got a heartbeat and a reason, I can train you. If all you've got is ego and an excuse? Good luck with that.

And here's the reality—especially in media: the look always lands before the message. Eyes decide before ears even bother. That's the way the system's wired.

I've told my male clients this more than once—especially the ones on camera. They'll ask what I thought about their segment, and I'll shrug:
"I couldn't tell you. I was too busy watching your form for what needs fixing."

They laugh. I'm not always kidding.

Because when it comes to showing up, men and women aren't playing from the same rulebook. Not on camera. Not in the boardroom. Not even in the gym.

And that's where the concealer comes in. Not the makeup kind. The kind that hides the shake in your hands, the catch in your breath, the fact that showing up at all takes more grit than anyone watching will ever give you credit for.

For him, presence is enough.
For her, presence has to come wrapped, polished, and ready for inspection before a word even lands.

253

Chapter 25: He Shows Up. She Arrives.

Because nothing says "credibility" like a fresh set of lashes
and a wrinkle-free forehead.

There's something hypnotic about the nightly news.
The cool confidence.
The steady eye contact.
The polished delivery that says, We know what we're
talking about. Trust us.

But if you're really watching—
really watching—
you'll notice something else.

A pattern.
A wrinkle in the wrinkle policy.

The men?
They're allowed to age.
Hell, they're expected to.

Every crease, every silver hair, every soft belly under the
tie—
it all adds up to that mythical quality called gravitas.

Silver at the temples? Distinguished.
A lined forehead? Experience.
A paunch? Relatable. Even charming.

But the women?
Oh, the rules are different.

You can be brilliant.
You can be assertive.
You can have a résumé that makes the Pulitzer committee
weep.

But you can't look tired.
Or puffy.
Or droopy.
Or real.

Or natural.
Or over 39.

You need a glow—but not a sheen.
A fullness—but never puffiness.
Lashes for days—but God forbid a rogue chin hair or a
single forehead line.

And the hair.
Oh, the hair.

Long, thick, silky—
blonde that somehow never turns brassy,
even after five rounds of highlights.

Hair that's been blow-dried, flat-ironed, curled, keratin-
treated, sprayed,
and fried under hot lights—
and still swishes like a shampoo commercial.

How?
Magic?
Money?

A glam squad armed with serums and prayers?
Wigs? Clip-ins?
A deal with the devil and a top-tier colorist?

I don't have a clue.

But I do know this:
That hair is part of the uniform.
Just like the lashes.
Just like the glow-but-not-sheen.
Just like the smile that says, Don't worry—I'm still soft
enough to be likable.

It's all part of the image required to keep the job.

The hair can't look tired, either.

It's a tightrope walk—
in full makeup,
under full lights,
with an invisible expiration date no one will admit exists—
but everyone knows is there.

And I've seen it. Up close.

I've trained women in media—
local, national, faces you'd recognize.

The pressure?
It's relentless.

Their workouts aren't just about health.
Or strength.

Or that feel-good rush of stress relief.

They're about optics.
Camera angles and contract renewals.

Their job security is skin-deep—literally.

They train to stay employable.
To shrink their waists.
To blur their lines.
To keep their seat at the anchor desk—
not just to feel strong,
but to stay visible,
valuable,
undeniable.

Meanwhile, I've trained a few men in media, too.
Still working.
Still prominent.
Still... wrinkled.

And not once—
not once—
have I heard a whisper about eye lifts or concealer.

Nobody's pulling them aside before a ratings period to
suggest they "freshen up their look."
Nobody's gently proposing a little Botox "just between us."

They show up with their opinions,
their suits,
and their extra chin.
And nobody blinks.

It's not that I want them held to the same ridiculous standard.
I just want the women freed from it.

Turn on any legacy news show—
something with a ticking stopwatch and a panel of men
who look like they've been reporting since the Cold War—
and tell me I'm wrong.

They've got wrinkles deep enough to map troop movements.
Age spots.
Gravity-tested jowls.
Hair that's turned every shade of gray—and then some.

And not only are they still on air—
they're revered.

Because somewhere along the line,
aging also became a credential.
At least for men.

They're not subjected to wardrobe consults with polite notes like,
"Try a lower neckline," or
"Could you wear your hair a little softer?"

They show up in suits—
sometimes just sport coats—
and that's that.

As if gravitas lives in the lapel.

One client, still active on camera,
had a habit of slumping at his desk mid-segment.
From the front, he looked authoritative enough.
But from the side?
His shoulders looked like they'd gone out for lunch without
him.

The camera angle doubled his belly,
turned him into a cautionary tale about posture—live.

And the studio?
Didn't say a word.

Not once.

You bet I did.

Can you imagine a woman getting that kind of silent pass?

Her posture would've been corrected before her mic was
even clipped on.
If she dared to slouch or looked bloated under bad lighting,
she'd be in someone's office before the commercial break
was over:
"We love you; we do... but viewers can be cruel."

I didn't help those women reclaim anything.
I just kept them strong
while they were still allowed to stay.

And then—just like that—
they were replaced.

Not all.
Some.

Not for lack of talent.
Not for lack of ratings.
For looking like they'd lived.

Which, of course, they had.

The men?
They stayed.
A couple, retired out.
Aging on camera right alongside the rest of us—
untouched,
unbothered,
and still taken seriously.

And don't even get me started on hair, again.
Though here I go.

Men can go silver,
salt-and-pepper,
full chrome dome—whatever.

It's "distinguished."
It adds "character."

There's that gravitas again.

Try that with a woman.

Try showing up with visible gray roots
and suddenly she's "let herself go."

Sure, there are exceptions.
Women who've carved out careers
without fitting the beauty algorithm.
But they're rare.
They're brilliant.
Often polarizing.

They've survived the system—
not been embraced by it.

And even then, more often than not,
they still look—surprised—youthful.
Because aging out is still a risk.
Even for the ones who've already earned their seat.

So no, I'm not here to bash men.
I'm just pointing out the obvious:

When a man walks on set
with crow's feet and a double chin,
he gets called "experienced."

When a woman shows up with the same?
She gets called a cab.

That's not bitterness.
That's bandwidth.

And I've spent a lifetime watching
who gets to stay in the frame—
and who's told to shrink until they vanish.

So yes, appearances matter.
More than they should.

But here's the thing:

When used right,
appearance isn't just vanity.
It's voice.

I learned that from Sunny.

Because before I ever taught a wide-leg squat,
or called out a slouch,
or watched women try to defend themselves
under the weight of a camera lens—

I watched Sunny.

And she showed me
that style isn't just what you wear.
It's how you refuse to disappear.

Chapter 26: Styled by Sunny

Somewhere between the spandex racks
and the Kennedy Center aisles, I realized something:

DC isn't exactly a fashion capital.
Hell, it's barely fashion-aware.

There, I said it.

Sure, you'll catch the occasional flash of flair—
an intern fresh from Manhattan,
or someone who wandered into a Zara on a brave day.
But for the most part?
DC dresses like it's permanently stuck in the TSA pre-check
line.

Sensible shoes. Uninspired hair.
A sea of neutral tones, elastic waistbands,
and jackets that scream function over everything.

I've seen beige cardigans with orthopedic shoes at galas.
Fleece vests at funerals.

Somewhere in a Georgetown closet,
there's a $1,200 handbag stuffed with Werther's Originals
and the fear of being judged for wearing color.

And the hair?
It matches the vibe—
safe, sensible, and just scared enough to avoid standing out.

So no, I won't apologize

for expecting more from the public display of self.

In a world that reduces us to parts—
weight, wrinkles, waistbands—
style is one of the few things we still get to choose.

Enter Sunny.

Sunny didn't step into the world of swimwear—
she built it.

From design tables to dressing rooms,
sketch pad to sales floor,
she touched every thread, every seam, every decision.

She didn't just create a business.
She created a presence.

When Sunny walked into a room—
whether it was a New York trade show
or a cluttered back stockroom in Bethesda—
you felt her before you saw her.

She didn't just dress bodies.
She sculpted confidence.

She gave shape to identity—
often before the person inside even knew who they were
becoming.

And me?
I wasn't just her mannequin.

I was her co-conspirator.
Her canvas.
Her living, breathing proof of concept.

It didn't hurt that our interests aligned—
and that nearly everything looked good on me.

Not because I was perfect,
but because I knew how to wear clothes—
and own them.

Even back then,
I understood what worked, what didn't,
and how to create the attitude I wanted
the moment I walked out the door.

But luck had nothing to do with it.

This was how our lives played out:
intertwined, expressive, occasionally explosive.

Even when we clashed (and we did),
our shared language held:

Clothing. Fabric. Form. Fit.
And the occasional full-throated,
"What the hell are you wearing?"

We became true friends
after I graduated from Oberlin.

Business partners, yes—
but bonded by something deeper:

The joy of assembling a look that didn't just work—
it spoke.

Not for money.
Not for approval.

For the thrill.
For the creativity.
For the attitude.

And maybe—
for the quiet, defiant pleasure of turning heads
in a town where heads rarely turn.

Our Fashion Adventures Took Flight in New York

The Manhattan swimwear markets?
Fast. Fierce. Unapologetic.

We thrived on that pace—darting from one showroom to
the next, grabbing what inspiration and opportunity the
city threw at us. It was chaos with a skyline, and Sunny
never missed a beat.

We'd hop cabs, catch a Broadway matinee,
devour something messy at a deli,
then prowl the garment district like it owed us something.

Sunny had a sixth sense for finding treasure in chaos—
leftover clothing samples, misprinted labels,
one-off runs of designer dreams that never made it to retail.

We'd finger the seams,
sneer at overdesigned disasters,
and then—boom—uncover a $19 gem
that looked like it fell off a runway.

Yeah, we'd stroll through them—
not to buy, but to see.
To know.

"Fortunoff's. Bergdorf's. Saks. Bloomingdale's."

Like spies in a hostile country,
gathering intel before returning to our suburban outpost,
armed with knowledge no one else had.

And I'll tell you what:
I felt more alive in those moments

than I ever did back home in DC.

The contrast was brutal.

At twenty-something,
I'd dress for the Kennedy Center on a Saturday night—
heels, a sleek outfit, a genuine attempt at glam.

And I'd be surrounded by couples in jeans.
Or worse—those stiff khakis
that pleat themselves into submission.

I once saw a guy in a windbreaker at the opera.
A windbreaker.

Restaurants?
Same story.

Places where the bill could make your credit card weep,
and the patrons looked like they'd just left Costco.

And look—
I am a Costco shopper.

I love knowing I've got 40 rolls of toilet paper,
and a paper towel tower jammed into my apartment closet
like it's fallout prep.

But come on.
There's a time and a place.

And dinner at a white-tablecloth steakhouse
isn't the moment for cargo shorts

and sneakers held together with hope.

Unless the place had a dress code—
and thankfully, a few still do.

Somewhere along the way,
DC confused "comfortable" with "acceptable"—
and style fell straight into the Potomac.

Sunny and me?
We were having none of it.

Fashion wasn't about money.

It was about meaning.

When Sunny and I had free time—real time, the kind not
hijacked by errands or obligation—we didn't go to the
movies. We didn't hit the park.

We went shopping.

Not in that frantic, fill-the-void way people shop when they
hate their closets—or their lives.

This was sport.
This was pleasure.
This was two women—one technically past her prime in
years (never in spark), the other still tuning her visual
voice—out to defy a city that dressed like it was afraid of
being noticed.

We'd hit funky little boutiques, off-the-wall secondhand shops, random clearance outlets—anywhere Sunny's Spidey-sense whispered there was buried treasure.

Sale racks first. Always.

And then?
We'd create.

We paired pieces like stylists on a deadline—mixing vintage with new, throwing in a bold shoe, adding just enough edge to make heads swivel.

Sometimes the looks were elegant.
Sometimes sexy.
Never trashy.
Always distinct.

That was the bar:
Show the best damn version of yourself. Always.
Whether the crowd got it or not.

Over the years, I've gone shopping with a friend or two.
Sweet people, don't get me wrong.

But most of them say, "That looks great!" the second I step out of the fitting room.

Why?
Because it fits. Because I'm lean and athletic. And that alone is often enough to impress people.

But not Sunny.

Sunny sees differently.
She doesn't care if it fits.
She cares if it speaks.

And if it doesn't?
She'll let me know in a way that makes me want to peel it off like poison ivy.

Most of her zingers are one-liners—brilliant, brutal, and gone before you can write them down.

But there's one she's used more than once, and trust me, it sticks:
"It has much more appeal on the hanger than on you."

Ouch.
And thank you.

Because she's usually right.

We still head out on these little retail missions.
Not always to buy—but we're not walking in blind, either.

The goal isn't spending.
It's looking. Creating. Feeling something click.

But if a piece jumps out that neither of us can resist?
Well. No arm-twisting required.

Take a recent trip to Forever 21, who by the way, is now "Out of Business."

Yes, we were "just looking."
Which, in our language, means look... perhaps try on... a possibility to purchase.

We stumbled on this little black number—sequins for days, long sleeves, scoop neck, barely any back to speak of. Mini. Major. Over the top.

And it fit. Like it had been waiting for me.

Sunny said, "Check the price tag."

"Oh Sunny," I said, "it's on sale. Four dollars and ninety-nine cents."

She didn't miss a beat.
"Buy it. I'll find you a place to wear it."

I haven't worn it yet.
But you can bet I will.

Breakfast at Parkway

These days, Sunny and I still make appearances—though our catwalk now starts at 7:59 AM outside a deli in suburban Maryland. Every Sunday. Rain or shine.

It's an old-school, no-frills, New York-style deli that's been plating blintzes and brisket since the early '60s. The walls haven't changed much since then—and thank God. This place isn't trendy. It's tradition. The closest you'll get to real NYC deli taste without crossing state lines.

And Sunny? She looks forward to it. Although? *"If we win the lottery? Please let's move to NYC! Real delis there."*

We roll in—literally.
I push her wheelchair through the doors at 8:00 sharp, and we head straight to our table, our waitress, our usual.

Now—before we go further—let's talk about the pickles.

Sunny is a half-sour girl. Not full-sour. Not those puckered-up salt bombs most delis dish out. She wants just-crisp-enough, cucumber-colored, subtle bite. Half. Sour.

And every single week? The waitress brings the wrong ones.

"Oh! Sorry!" she says, as if surprised for the tenth time.

This last visit, I finally clarified:
"Look, the half-sours are the ones that still look like cucumbers."

She got it. Finally.
A small win in a world of endless corrections.

Sunny starts with those pickles—then gets serious:
Cheese blintzes, warm from the oven, with sour cream on the side.

Then comes the nova platter: thin slices of smoked salmon over romaine, with tomato, red onion, capers, olives, grapes, and cream cheese—plus a lightly toasted plain bagel, sliced just right. Nothing sloppy.

Me? Just an omelet. And coffee.

I'm not there for the food.
I'm there for the outfit.

That's right.
We dress up for deli breakfast.

While the regulars roll in wearing their Sunday not-so-finest—sweatshirts, worn sneakers, fleeces held together by a prayer—we show up like it's opening night at Café Carlyle.

Some of the pieces we've scored on our shopping adventures? We wear them.
No occasion required.

Sunny calls it a mashup of two classics: Breakfast at Tiffany's meets A Walk in the Park.

But really? It's neither.

It's Breakfast at Parkway Deli.

We get stares.
Some curious. Some confused.
A few approving nods from older women who get it.

Sometimes one leans over and says, "You look lovely today," and Sunny beams like she's back in a Manhattan showroom.

But I'm not there for the compliments.

I'm there because this is who we are. Still.

Because style isn't about who's watching—it's about showing up as the best damn version of yourself.

And Sunny? Even at 100 years old, she still shows up.

And there's nothing more fitting than that.

Flashback: Pickled in Transit

Years ago, when Sunny had to hold down the swimwear store, I'd fly solo to New York twice a month for market fill-ins and manufacturer visits. Our store manager, at times, could not work all available hours. And between business? I'd roam.

I love New York. Always have.

One afternoon, I was wandering Delancey Street when I spotted a long line curling around the block. Silly me, I thought, Cinnabon? It was that kind of era—malls were big, cinnamon buns were 'in'.

Around this same time "Crossing Delancey" was showing in theaters. And here I was on the lower east side of New York. I should have put two and two together.

But no. This wasn't pastry.

This was the motherland.

The original pickle maker of the Lower East Side. Barrels and barrels of pickles and tomatoes, swimming in brine, ready to be scooped into containers for lucky city dwellers— or, in this case, a devoted daughter.

My dad liked full-sours. Sunny, half-sours. I bought a container of each. With juice, of course. It never occurred to me that the juice might not stay in the container.

I hailed a cab to the airport—tight on time but optimistic.

Halfway through the ride?
Pickle juice. All. Over. Me.

It soaked my lap, my thighs, the cab seat, my clothes. And guess what? No napkins. No towels. Just me, stewing in a briny swamp, hoping my flight wasn't delayed, praying the smell read deli chic instead of strange body odor.

The cabbie didn't yell. I gave him a big tip and an apology.

No one at the gate said anything, but the people seated next to me on the flight gave me a few long looks.

What can I say?
I reeked of love. And vinegar.

Fashion isn't frivolous. It isn't shallow.

It's a declaration.
It's your armor. Your flirtation. Your fight song.

And I learned that from a woman who could style a mannequin better than half of DC could dress themselves.

"You don't dress to impress. You dress to express. And if someone doesn't get it? That's their fashion problem, not yours."

And if you're wondering what all this has to do with personal training?

Everything.

Because before I could train others to show up as their best selves,
I had to learn how to dress—and live—as mine.

I did.
Still do.
Now it's their turn.

Because not all judgment wounds.
Some of it stitches you back together—one perfectly chosen outfit at a time.

So, when I see a woman on screen wearing a swan as a scarf or a blazer made of sequins and sheer nerve, I don't laugh.
I take notes.

So yeah, style matters.

Not because it pleases the world,
but because it reminds you—every time you catch your reflection—

that you're alive, present, and unafraid to take up space.

And if you think that's shallow, you're not paying attention.

Because there's power in showing up exactly as you want to be seen—
even if it makes people uncomfortable.
Especially if it does.

Chapter 27: The Tutu Is My Offense

Yes, I know the clothes are far from practical.
Yes, I know Carrie would've filed bankruptcy by season two.

But there's something magnetic about watching women
who take up space—visually, emotionally, unapologetically.

They strut through their cities, their crises, their
heartbreaks, wearing outfits most people wouldn't dare
attempt outside of a runway or a themed charity gala.

And for the most part? Though there are times...
They're not dressing to attract a significant other.
They're not even dressing for each other.
They're dressing like they belong in a moment they
dreamed up—and then owned.

That's the power.
That's the joy.
That's the spell these shows cast.

You don't have to copy them.
You just have to feel the jolt of freedom they represent.

And that jolt?
It doesn't just come from a pair of Manolos or a feathered
jacket.
Sometimes, it comes from saying yes to something
ridiculously joyful.
Even when it's messy.
Especially when it's messy.

I devour every episode the way I devour a chocolate éclair from Vaccaro's in Little Italy, Baltimore—a once-in-a-blue-moon indulgence I didn't expect to fall for but did.

I'm not a dessert person. Never have been.
But those éclairs?
They're not dessert. They're an event.

I remember one Sunday, Sunny and I decided to split one on the drive home.

The thing was massive—nearly the size of a dinner plate, loaded with thick chocolate on top, and stuffed with enough rich custard to count as a second passenger.

We grabbed a couple of flimsy plastic forks, laughed at the futility of them, and went for it anyway.

She tried to feed me while I drove. I tried to time bites between traffic lights.

There was chocolate on my lap, custard on my shirt, and at one point, she missed my mouth entirely and I ended up with éclair on my nose.

We howled with laughter the whole way home—sticky, happy, completely unbothered.

That's how I watch these shows.
Not because I want to be those women—
but because they remind me it's okay to show up exactly how you want.

Fully. Boldly. Joyfully.
Even if you ruin your shirt in the process.

Personally?
I've been inspired by more of Carrie's outfits than I'd ever admit—
scratch that, I would admit it.

Happily. Loudly.
In line at the DMV if necessary.

No, I can't afford the originals.
But give me a good knock-off, a vintage twist, and the right dose of don't-give-a-damn?
It gets the job done.

And yes, I've caught those looks—
the "Who does she think she is?" glances.

You know the ones or perhaps you don't.

And yes, I kept walking.
Probably with better posture.

"Who says you can't wear sequins, a corset, and faux fur
next to a Christmas tree?
Watch me."

Because here's what people may not be thinking:
When you wear something bold, something joyful,
something "too much,"
you're not just putting on clothes.
You're putting on nerve.
You're putting on permission.
You're stepping into a version of yourself that doesn't ask
for approval—
and won't wait around for it anyway.

And those shows—those over-the-top, feather-adorned,
beret-wearing, rhinestone-laced fever dreams?
They remind us there's power in that.

For all the people who mock Emily in Paris—and yes, she's
ridiculous—
they're still watching.

Why?
Because deep down, we all want to know what she's going
to wear next.
We want to see someone go for it.
Full throttle.
No filter.

It's fantasy, sure—but it's fantasy with consequences.
Clothes that start conversations.
Outfits that piss people off.
Characters who live like their wardrobe matters—
which, surprise: it does.

And let's not forget The Marvelous Mrs. Maisel.
Different decade, same magic.
The woman storms through chaos wrapped in jewel tones
and grit.
Every coat is a declaration.
Every dress, an act of defiance.

She may be unraveling inside,
but outside?
She's draped in dignity and a lipstick shade that could stop
traffic.

And then there's The Gilded Age.
If you want a masterclass in wearing your space,
watch these characters sweep through drawing rooms and
horse-drawn streets,
layered in silks and feathers, top hats and corsets,
jewels catching the gaslight as they move.

The women take up space, sure—
but so do the men,
striding through scenes with canes and confidence,
coats cut to precision, hats worn like crowns.
This includes the working classes structured throughout.
They all wear their status, their ambition, their power—on
purpose.

And it's not just costume drama.
It's a reminder that how you show up in the world
signals how you feel about yourself—
even when the world is ready to judge you for it.

I don't care what decade you're in—
that kind of presentation still slaps.

Some call it frivolous.
I call it strategy.

The clothes are never just clothes.
They're armor.
Identity.
A subtle middle finger to anyone who underestimates you.
They say, "This is who I am—even if the world hasn't caught
up yet."

And what do all these women have in common?
They're not trying to blend.
They're not aiming for relatable.
They're going for unforgettable.

And whether you love them or loathe them, that's why you
keep watching.

So no, I may never wear a ballgown to brunch.
And no, I'm not swanning through Paris in a chartreuse
feathered shrug.

But I will show up.
In color.
In confidence.
In something that makes it damn clear:
I didn't just roll out of someone else's expectations.

Because I was raised by a woman who believed in tailoring,
in presence,
in showing up like you meant it.

Sunny didn't blindly follow trends—
but she tracked them like a hunter.

She had to.
In retail, it mattered.
Clients wanted to know what was in, what was next, what
everyone else was chasing.

But when it came to her own compass?
She steered toward transformation.

She knew that when someone slipped into the right suit—
the right cut, the right feel—
their spine straightened.
Their voice came forward.
They stopped apologizing for their body
and started inhabiting it.

That's what these shows get right, beneath all the sequins
and sass.
They remind us—especially women—
that being visible is a risk.
But it's also a right.

That dressing for yourself
can be the most radical thing you do all day.

And sometimes?
You wear that frivolous tutu.

Not because it's practical.
Because it's yours.

Dressing others?
It started as our job.
But I made it an art.

Sunny didn't just fit suits.
She helped women step into themselves.
And I took it further—
using fit and fabric to help people see themselves,
often before they were ready to.

Nowhere was that work more intense, more unpredictable,
or more revealing than inside—
And trust me,
each coast had its own attitude—
and its own stories worth telling.

Chapter 28: From Showrooms to Sales Floor

Some women dream of front-row seats at Paris Fashion Week.
Me? I got my adrenaline in New York's swimwear showrooms and the wide, generous sprawl of the L.A. markets.

Sunny and I didn't just run a store—we ran a year-round command center for Lycra, shelf bras, and seasonal urgency.

Swimwear wasn't just product. It was personal. It brought out armor, attitude, and everything women carried underneath.

Sure, we sold sundresses, wraps, tees, skirts, sunglasses— whatever made summer easier to wear.

But the suits?
That was where the pressure lived. That was the buy we had to get right.

To stay ahead, we had to see the full lines early—before reps rolled in with curated racks and over-rehearsed pitches.

Manufacturers sent them to us a few times a year, wheeling in suits like stock portfolios.

But the real decisions, the real insight?
That happened in the showrooms.

Sunny, early 1990s, NYC.
We didn't go to Bergdorf's to shop. We went to watch—
fabric, fashion, attitude.

New York was business.
Fast-paced. No-nonsense.
A million suits to see, prices to negotiate, delivery dates to lock down before your competition did.

But for all its hustle, New York knew how to treat its customers.

The showrooms were stocked—sandwiches, sodas, cookies. Maybe even a crumbly biscotti if you got lucky. You'd grab a plate, scan the racks while chewing, nod to a rep across the room, and kept moving. Fast, but still human.

Gottex—one of the heavy hitters at the time—hosted full-on runway shows, usually at a fashion center in the city, maybe Parsons. I can't say for sure.

But what I do remember?
The room. The legs.

The hushed rustle of industry women—and more than a few men—trying to look bored while secretly clocking the one suit that would vanish the second it hit a real body.

Some of those models? They'd end up in Sports Illustrated's swimsuit issue.

That always triggered its own kind of backstage frenzy.
The reps would name-drop.
The buyers would pretend not to care.
And somewhere between the flashbulbs and the fabrics, the politics of who got which suit first played out like fashion chess.

Every spring, like clockwork, customers would march into our store with Sports Illustrated in hand, manicured finger jabbing at page 62.

And it wasn't just women.

Men would show up with that same issue, asking—no, expecting—to see every suit featured inside so they could "buy one for their girlfriend."

It was always girlfriend.
Never once did a guy say it was for his wife.

And of course, we didn't carry most of the suits from those pages.

Those were editorial fantasies—gimmick pieces cut for models with eight-foot-long legs and the physics-defying ability to keep a suit in place while rolling in the surf.

They weren't designed for mortals.

But that didn't stop women from asking.

"I want this one."
"Do you have just the top half?"
"Will this work on me?"

No, no, and sweetie—not unless you've got the bone structure of a whittled wishbone and a torso like that model, who, by the way, once told me she downed vodka before swimsuit shoots just to loosen up.

She was the cover girl that year. Paulina.

Earthy, funny, totally honest. Not a diva—just real.

She laughed as she told me about the shoot.

"Char, I swear—ten thousand shots just to get one that makes me look that good. One day I had a zit on my nose, and the photographers acted like the world was ending. A goddamn zit!"

And yes—they airbrushed it.

This was back when airbrushed was still whispered like a trade secret—
not tapped casually on your phone under "Smooth Skin" or "AI Enhance."

The editing took hours.
The illusion? Two seconds.
The public? Hooked.

Gottex kept the runway magical—long legs, glossy hair, suits that looked poured on.

But the real magic?
That happened on our sales floor.

Where suits met skin without an entourage.
Where we worked in reality, not retouching.
Where the fantasy met the mirror—
and we still found a way to make it work.

The Contrast — Let's Talk About the L.A. Markets

In New York, if you dressed up, no one blinked.
Heels, jacket, tailored pants—expected. Required.
The uniform of someone who came to play and planned to win.

You moved fast, kept notes, placed orders.

Maybe—maybe—you were offered a flute of something bubbly.
But only after you'd committed to five dozen units in four color ways.

It was business.
Fast, loud, layered, and often hilarious—
especially when sugar got involved.

Then came Los Angeles.

Walk into an L.A. showroom in your polished, New York-ready outfit, and the first thing you'd hear was:
"Whoa—what are you dressed up for? Relax."

Relax? We were on the clock.

Before a single suit hit the rack, they wanted to know:
"Where are you staying?"
"Did you try that new place in Venice?"
"Have you been to Malibu Country Mart yet?"
"How's your vibe?"

The pace? Slower. Softer.
Smiles that lasted a beat too long.
Conversations that lingered.

And while Sunny and I weren't your stereotypical aggressive New Yorkers, this whole let's chat first, maybe do business later—or not at all energy?

It took a minute.
Or a day.
Two, if the hotel pillows were bad.

We'd fake it for diplomacy's sake—
nodding at kombucha samples, tossing out vague sushi
recommendations.

But the second we were back in the car?
Pacific Coast Highway or bust.

Zuma Beach. Santa Monica. Ocean air. Actual movement.

Not to shop. Not to schmooze.
Just to keep our legs moving and our eyes off another
showroom rep saying:
"These run a little small, but they're super cute if you have
the right body."

We didn't come to be cute.
We came to order.

Back in New York, things were different—
faster, sharper, and occasionally... family-infused.

There was one trip Sunny couldn't make.
Our trusted manager was out sick, and someone had to
watch the store, again.

So, I flew solo.

Well, almost solo.

My cousin, a cardiologist doing research at Johns Hopkins, asked if he could tag along.

"I want to see what it's like," he said, wide-eyed and curious.

"Fine. Be my assistant for a couple days," I replied.

I should've known better.

He was polite. Professional.
For about ten minutes.

Then we hit the showrooms—during Fashion Week, no less—and the man turned into a teenage boy let loose in a Vegas revue.

He didn't say anything gross. He didn't leer.
But the sparkle in his eyes when those showroom models strutted past in high-cut Gottex showstoppers?
Blinding.

"Oh, that one's interesting," he murmured, trying to sound analytical.

"Ask her to turn around—look at the back detailing."

Back detailing, my ass.

I let him enjoy the view.

And truth be told, some of those suits were standouts.

I even ordered one or two based on his reactions.

Not because I was taking fashion advice from a guy in scrubs—
but because I trusted my instincts.

If a conservative cardiologist from Baltimore perked up,
I knew a few of our DC clients might too.

Later that night, back at the hotel, he tried to act like it was all very academic.
"Very educational," he said, sipping a minibar drink like he'd just completed a fellowship in Lycra Studies.
"A whole other side of anatomy."

I rolled my eyes.
"You're lucky Sunny wasn't here. She'd have smacked the cardiologist right out of you."

And she would've—
right after asking which suits drew the most attention,
which reps were peddling last year's rejects,
and whether anyone looked desperate enough to deal.

That trip reminded me:
Swimwear retail isn't just about fabric and fit.

It's endurance.
It's walking ten thousand steps across concrete showrooms,
squinting at neon prints under punishing lights,
mentally calculating which suits would actually sell—
and which only looked good on a Sports Illustrated cover
soaked in Photoshop.

Some people fantasize about front-row seats at Fashion Week.
Me?
I learned to survive on phenomenal New York bagels and runway adrenaline,
placing thousand-dollar orders while making sure no one passed out from low blood sugar.

Because this wasn't a hobby.
It was business.

And the hustle?
It never looked good in soft focus.

There were other markets, of course—Miami among them—
bright colors, bold suits, body-forward displays.
It had its moments.
But it didn't pull us the same way.

We weren't there for the spectacle.
We were there to stock a store for real women, with real lives and real bodies—
and help them find a suit that made them feel like they belonged in the spotlight, too.

And as for the sales reps who came directly to the store throughout the year?
Ugh.

Too one-on-one. Too performative.

Most were men—

and most walked in with the confident energy of someone who thought he knew better.

They'd unfurl their rolling racks like Broadway curtains and launch into the same tired pitch:
"This one's a bestseller."
"This one's moving fast."
"Everyone's ordering this color."

Oh really?
Everyone?

Let me be crystal clear:
At the time, there were very few swimwear-only retailers—especially in the mid-Atlantic or D.C. metro area.

We weren't just some seasonal display crammed next to the sale sundresses.
We were the swimwear department.

We recognized how a woman held herself—the breath she paused, the arms that stayed folded, the way she glared back at the mirror like it had betrayed her.

We saw the stiffness, the hesitation, the quiet calculation: Is it the suit? Or is it me?

We knew that moment.
And we didn't flinch.

You'd hear it sometimes—quiet, tentative:
"Is it me?"

Not dramatic. Not loud.
Just a woman standing in a swimsuit she didn't ask to feel
judged by, trying to make sense of the mirror.
Holding her breath.
Blaming her body.

And the reps?
The ones wheeling in racks, tossing out lines about
bestsellers and trending colors like they knew what women
really needed?
Most had never seen what we saw every day.

Never stood beside someone frozen in front of her
reflection.
Never had to say, "It's not your body. It's the cut."

Even in the New York showrooms, you'd see tables reserved
for major department store buyers—
young women from Nordstrom or Saks, perched with
notebooks, picking suits for entire regions.

And I'd think:
Really? Who exactly are you buying for?

Because unless you've worked the actual swimsuit section—
fielded the meltdowns, the demands, the double
mastectomy fittings, the post-baby self-esteem collapses—
how the hell do you know what to buy?

And don't even get me started on the manufacturers' reps
swooping in to kiss their asses and push certain lines for
maximum numbers.

Forget fit. Forget logic.
It was all about the size of the order and the softness of the
buyer.

So yeah—we preferred the showrooms.
For the frenzy.
For the candy trays.
For the occasional runaway model story.

But mostly?
For the full picture.

We saw it all.
We knew what our clients would want.
And we ordered like we meant it.

Because unlike those buyers perched in borrowed chairs,
we didn't just observe bodies.
We worked with them.
Every single day.

And here's the part that still blows my mind:
Most of the sales reps—whether in the store or in the
showrooms—were men.

Men, representing manufacturers, selling suits they'd never
have to wear.

I'm not some card-carrying feminist with a megaphone.
But how in the hell is a man supposed to understand what
it feels like
to walk into a dressing room, half-naked under fluorescent
lights,

wearing spandex that exposes everything you've spent a
lifetime trying to manage, ignore, or make peace with?

They couldn't.

But they sure knew how to pitch.

And the truth is—when the suits came off?
That's when the real stories began.

Not catalog stories.
Not beach fantasies or size-tag illusions.
Just people.
Flawed, funny, fiercely human.

So, let's leave the sales floor behind.
The bright lights.
The mirror panic.
The racks that never stopped groaning.

Let's walk into the sessions.
Into the rhythm. The banter.
The push-pull of effort and trust.

Into the spaces where people show up—
sometimes tired, sometimes fired up, always human.

Where progress isn't just pounds lost or inches dropped,
but confidence gained—
and the quiet decision to keep going.

Because this is where the real work lives.
Not in the fabric.
In the fight.

Not in the fitting room.
In the muscle—and the will behind it.

Once the suits were gone,
the work—and the stories—moved from the sales floor
to the training floor.

Where showing up was only the beginning.

Think of this as the ground floor.
Volume Two climbs higher—into everything those
experiences shaped: how I work, who I train, the rules I
broke, and the lives that collided with mine because of it.

What's ahead isn't just a next chapter.
It's the real story.